Letters

to

JEWISH
COLLEGE
STUDENTS

BY THEODORE FRIEDMAN

JONATHAN DAVID -- Publishers -- New York

LETTERS TO
JEWISH COLLEGE STUDENTS

by Theodore Friedman

Copyright 1965 by
JONATHAN DAVID/PUBLISHERS

Library of Congress Catalogue Card No. 65–17362

No part of this book may be reproduced
in any manner without written
permission from the publishers. Address all inquiries to:
JONATHAN DAVID/PUBLISHERS
131 East 23rd Street, New York, N.Y. 10010

Type set at The Polyglot Press
Printed in the United States of America

For the Young People of Beth El
In Confidence and Hope

Table of Contents

Preface

THIS volume is the fruit of a project carried on by the author in the congregation to which he has been privileged to minister this past decade. Monthly, during the college year, I directed a fairly brief informal discussion of some aspect of Judaism in the form of a letter to the college students of my congregation. Almost invariably these letters were intended as answers to questions on Judaism in its contemporary meaning that presumably troubled young people. Their epistolary form dictated their informality of style and direct form of address, both of which elements have been retained in the present volume. Encouraged by the interest and response—the latter, often, in the form of further questions on the part of the original recipients of these letters—I am emboldened to assemble these messages in book form in the hope that they can speak convincingly to a larger audience of Jewish college students, as well as to others who may be seeking answers to questions that have been disturbing them.

While I have made no effort to present a systematic in-clusive exposition of Jewish doctrine and practice, the letters have been so ordered as to follow a fairly definite sequence of ideas. These, in their range, cover the basic themes of any contemporary interpretation of Judaism. Throughout, the exposition has been directed to the mind and spirit challenged by modern knowledge and culture toward a more mature understanding of Judaism. If this book should help its readers reach a deepened loyalty to, and appreciation of, Jewish religion and the tradition, I shall feel myself more than amply rewarded.

THEODORE FRIEDMAN

Chanukah 5725
Jerusalem, Israel

1

**The
Meaning
Of
Faith**

I WARRANT that you have had the experience of occasionally taking the wrong turn while driving a car. The further
you drove, the further you found yourself from your destina-
tion. All roads do not lead to Rome, or whatever our specific
objective might be.

I cite this simple, familiar experience in order to indicate
that every goal has its own appropriate approach. One ought
be generally mindful of this elemental fact and most
especially when one reflects on that which is *sui generis*—
the existence of God. It is in this light, that I approach the
oft-repeated challenge: "Prove the existence of God."

I insist that, in the ordinary meaning of that term, proof
is no more appropriate to grasping the reality of God than
dark glasses are to viewing a Rembrandt painting. I am
aware, of course, that many penetrating minds, in the course
of several thousand years of human speculation, have made
the attempt. But always, the results, while impressive, have
lacked finality. Even more importantly, the proofs for God's
existence have always struck me as radically irrelevant. The
basic religious claim and demand are pointed towards faith
in God, not proof of God.

3

Consider the vast distinctions between the two. Proof is appropriate to that which is an object, a thing, or a process. Verification must ultimately be possible in terms of experimentation that can be performed by anyone and repeated as often as desirable. Clearly, God conceived as an object, finite and subject to experimentation, is not God but an idol, a thing, or a being among other things or beings. Hence, the biblical injunction against the making of physical images or, for that matter, mental pictures of God.

But what if, as is the case, one conceives of God as infinite being, as He who encompasses all that is or can be or, as the old, beautiful phrase of the prayer-book puts it, "the Life of all Worlds."

Proof is as irrelevant as it is, in the strict sense of the term, impossible. One cannot prove that on which all proof is based—existence and its infinite ground. (A subsequent Letter will deal with the nature of that infinite ground or, in simple terms, how we ought to conceive of God.)

There is, however, an even more far-reaching distinction between faith and proof. In certain specific, limited areas, a prudent person would not act, under normal circumstances, except on the basis of proof. (No one would take a drug whose effects, both positive and negative, had not been thoroughly pre-tested.) The broader enterprises of life, those which involve our total being, cannot await positive proof before their launching, for such proof can never in the nature of things ever be forthcoming. Two young people may resolve to embark upon marriage certain that it will bring them mutual happiness and self-fulfillment. There are grounds for their certainty: their love for one another, the mutual understanding they have already found, etc. But certainly,

4

there can be no proof in any real meaning of that word, that they will be happy. It is a venture. Similarly, there are grounds for having faith in God, but there can be no proof. (I will be talking about those grounds in subsequent letters. This letter is concerned with Faith.)

So, then, faith in God is essentially a venture which, if taken seriously, can affect our total life: our attitude towards society and its problems, and towards the way life ought to be lived. While faith in God can thus undergird our life, and is, therefore, all encompassing, its essential nature can be illustrated from three universal human enterprises, the pursuit of truth, goodness and beauty.

In the pursuit of truth we start from something that cannot really be proved: that the world is intelligible and amenable to human reason. If this confidence were to crumble, the central nerve of all intellectual activity would be severed. But as man proceeds in his quest of truth he becomes increasingly aware that the task is an endless one. The world to be known is inexhaustible. There is no area of human knowledge of which it may be said that its limits have been, or can be, reached. If there were limits, we would quickly lose one of the great impelling motives for the search: the joy of discovery.

Similarly, in the moral life faith is necessarily involved. Expediency, personal interest, or immediate advantage all would prompt us occasionally to tamper with truth, justice and compassion. What is it but faith in these that impels us to exercise them and damn the consequences? What kind of proof can there be that justice is better than injustice? Better for whom? Thus, the moral life, too, is at bottom a venture of faith, a deliberate choice of attitudes and actions beyond

5

the reach of proof. (Incidentally, if we could prove the moral life superior to the immoral, and there are those who claim to have achieved the feat, would such proof make people act in an ethical fashion? No more than proof of God's existence would make people religious.) A truly moral man damns the consequences to himself, though at the same time he is confident that ultimately his moral act will be vindicated. In a word, he has faith.

Even in the realm of art, the pursuit of beauty, an element of faith is involved—the faith that there is beauty in the world that can be actualized in creative artistic endeavor. But always there is the realization that it is never fully possible to grasp and completely render that beauty in all its infinite reach. The world of beauty discloses itself. Yet more remains hidden than is actually revealed. One recalls Keats' lines from his "Ode To a Grecian Urn".

"Heard melodies are sweet,
but those unheard are sweeter."

In each of these realms, then, faith is not simply hypothesis, a probability arrived at by weighing alternatives, but possesses rather an aspect of the compelling. One feels compelled to search for truth, obliged to choose the good and eschew the evil, impelled to create and admire the beautiful. There is, besides, the realization that always there is a beyond which forever eludes our finest spun net of thought, even as it eludes our best moral and aesthetic powers.

If this be the nature of faith, a venture of one's entire being that, as we have seen, draws forth man's highest powers, what can the venture of faith in God elicit from man? The answer to that question depends, of course, on how we conceive of God. A commitment to truth brings forth knowledge,

6

a commitment to the moral life brings forth acts of goodness, a commitment to beauty brings forth art. What does the commitment—or faith—in God bring forth? What are we committing ourselves to when we say, "I believe in God?" Or, very simply, "Who is God?" To that question, I shall return in my next Letter.

In the meantime, all I have attempted to do here, is to point out that proof never really brought anyone to a deep, authentic awareness of God. Faith does and can.

*The
Sickness
Of
Our
Time*

THE UNENDING multiplication of mechanical gadgets—literally, even teaching machines—readily gives rise to the delusion that our modern life is all sheer gain. More education, better health, more leisure, an ever-widening spread of life's necessities, and even luxuries—in all this, certainly at first glance, one hardly detects a note of deprivation.

I write you, however, to take a closer, more critical view, one motivated not by a hypercritical attitude, but rather by a broader and more realistic perspective. Something supremely precious is fading away from the consciousness of modern man, something so basic that no amount of advance in education, health, leisure, etc., can ever compensate for its loss. Indeed, the day it vanishes completely, George Orwell's 1984 will be upon us—the mechanical world in which man will have been utterly drained of his humanity and reduced to an organic puppet, manipulated much as we now manipulate and "set" electronic computers.

That something, is man's sense of the holy. That sense, I aver, is an innate human capacity, as innate and as distinct as man's capacity for response to the beautiful, or his capacity

8

to respond to right and wrong, or truth and falsehood.

Like all basic human potentials, it cannot be adequately defined, but that it is real and has played a central, civilizing, humanizing role in the development of man, cannot be denied. What the holy is in itself, one can hardly say, anymore than one can neatly pin down what constitutes the beautiful, per se. But our response to both is unmistakeable. What man considers holy he regards and approaches with awe and humility. To use it for one's own private purpose is to defile and desecrate it. I would say that it springs from the ever-present human recognition that there is something in the universe, infusing the world and transcending it, that points, beyond itself, to the source of all being. And it is over against that source that man ultimately stands.

So, then, in the course of history, man has attributed holiness to a bewildering variety of natural phenomena and objects, holy mountains, holy rivers, sacred animals, etc. Central to the tradition of the Western World, and springing from the Hebraic element within it, is the notion that there is something sacred about the human person. (The Hebraic element goes back to the verse in Genesis: "In the image of God, created He man.") There is no stage of human civilization, no matter how primitive, in which man did not, in some fashion, express his feeling for the aura of sanctity that surrounded the individual.

With the withering of the sense of the holy in modern times, it was inevitable that eventually human life itself would be downgraded, until man lost his status of person with a sacred inviolable center, and became a thing, an object to use or abuse, to manipulate or liquidate, whichever served one's purpose best at the moment.

9

Neither Fascism nor Communism (not Marxism) can be understood except against the background of this psychological revolution. Does anything, for example, sound more old-fashioned in our day than Kant's imperative: "Never treat man as a means, but always as an end?" Where is a man regarded as an end in himself rather than a means? In industry? On Madison Avenue?

What human misery or tragedy will not our press exploit for the sake of a journalistic scoop? Indeed, there are those who, for the sake of profit, are prepared to let the sacred experiences of their lives be exploited like freaks at a carnival. (Actual wedding ceremonies performed on television.)

To me, this loss of the sacred so manifest, for example, in the exhibitionism typical of current literature is the major sickness of society. Actually, there is no aspect of life that remains untainted by it: literature, politics, economics, morals.

To me, there is no more urgent and necessary task in our times than our recovery of the sense of the sacred. Begin by asking yourself, what do you regard as holy, so holy, that you would not dare use it for pleasure or profit, so holy that you approach it with awe, reverence and humility?

What Time Cannot Change

RECENTLY, our community celebrated its Centennial. Among the plethora of events celebrating the occasion there was one, in which I participated, that induces a speculative mood. On the grounds of the local high school, a Time Capsule, containing a variety of contemporary documents was buried. The capsule is meant to be opened a century hence.

The questions these proceedings raise are fairly obvious. What, of contemporary civilization, will endure to the year 2061? Of our contemporary life, as reflected in these documents, which include such items as comic books, taxpayers' lists, tape-recordings, etc., what will appear remote and outmoded?

May I hazard an educated guess? Our material civilization, its science and technology, as incorporated in the houses we now live in, the kind of transportation we use, the way we practice medicine, the way we manufacture things, virtually every object about us, will have undergone revolutionary changes, such changes, for example, that separate the horse and buggy from the jet plane.

Is this to say that all life is constant change, inexorably subject to the gnawing tooth of time?

11

I venture to suggest that that is but one aspect of life's panorama. There is another aspect, not less, but more significant than its transiency. Consider that aspect by starting with a few simple observations drawn from our everyday experience.

Here you are at college in the seventh decade of the 20th century, still reading and pondering the words of men like Plato, Aristotle, Aeschylus, St. Augustine, Milton, Shakespeare, the latest of whom lived over four hundred years ago. Will college students a century hence still be reading the same books? The question answers itself.

Not long ago, a single oil painting displayed at the Metropolitan Museum of Art, Rembrandt's "Aristotle Contemplating the Bust of Homer," drew 20,000 people in a single day, the largest crowd ever to visit the Museum in one day.

Rembrandt's painting is 300 years old. Granted that it endures physically, we may safely assume that a hundred, nay, five hundred years from now, people will still be contemplating that picture in rapt, reverential awe.

The examples may be multiplied but they all add up to this: There are indeed aspects of human experience and achievement which outlast the multiplying years. And among these, we submit, is man's eternal quest for the Reality that stands behind all reality. Will man outgrow religion? Man would first have to outgrow himself.

The psychologists tell us, and the evidence they advance is convincing, that there are certain images in the human unconscious that are eternal. We find these images in the designs and pictorial patterns of primitive man, and we find them in our own dream images today.

Even more: Human desires, as opposed to human wants,

12

have hardly changed within recorded human history. The Bible attests to that. Man desires love and courage and peace and freedom. He did three thousand years ago, and we opine that he will three thousand years hence.

In brief, life's material aspect is subject to all the fleeting impermanence of time. Life's spiritual aspect moves in slow wide swaths that sweep above the ever twisting and turning river of time. That, ultimately, is what the Psalmist meant when he said: "A thousand years in Thy sight are but as yesterday when it is past."

The Hidden Depths

To ME, a most important implication of man's current exploration of outer space is the revelation it has brought so vividly of the boundlessness of our universe. For all the heights that have been achieved and the discoveries of the nature of the atmosphere that surrounds this spinning globe, always there has come back the report that all these are but the outer edges of a universe that reaches beyond human conception.

I am suddenly reminded of the Prophet Isaiah's vision of God in which he sees the "hem of His garment filling the Temple"; that is, the outer reaches of God. Or, this comes to mind: Moses' confrontation with God in which the Prophet and Lawgiver is told that he will be permitted to see the "back of God but not His face."

And yet, because none of us can see the face of God, we find it difficult to conceive of God, and are reluctant to affirm His reality. To me, the hiddenness and obscurity of God are the most compelling elements in His reality.

What kind of a universe would it be if the mind of man could traverse it, from end to end, and see through it, from top to bottom? If the human mind could wrest every last

14

secret from nature, diagram it down to the last detail, express its operations from the chemistry of the blood to the chemistry and physics of the stars, the moon and the sun, we may be sure that the world would lose its fascination for us. But, of course, the proposition is utterly hypothetical, since every pushing forward of the frontiers of human knowledge always reveals leagues upon leagues of distant, unexplored horizons. The ancient Greek scientists, for example, thought they had the nature of the physical world completely diagrammed. It consisted, they said, of four elements: air, fire, earth and water. When I was in college I was taught that there were 88 elements. Since then, many new elements have been added to the atomic table.

So, the unknown remains a persistent aspect of reality, and it is this dimension that prods our minds to attempt further discovery, that fascinates us and attracts us. Nor is it otherwise in the realm of human nature. What, for example, is the power of friendship, the power that again and again draws us to our friend and impels us to seek his company? It is the fact that no matter how well we know and understand him, we always sense in him unrevealed depths of personality. Every human being is in that sense infinite. There is no one whom we can know and understand through and through. If we did, we would be bored by such a person. It is the unplumbed and unfathomed depths of the human personality that make up its endless fascination.

These two realms of human experience—of physical and human nature—point to the realm of man's experience and knowledge of God. God is both revealed and hidden, revealed in the world's order, intelligibility and beauty, and hidden in all the seeming senselessness and meaninglessness that

15

we experience and observe. How could it be otherwise? A God completely revealed, available for diagrammatic exposition, would hardly be a real God anymore than a person or a universe utterly defined and explained would be a real person or world. The French put it well: *Dieu defini est Dieu fini*—God defined is the end of God.

Every genuine religious spirit knew that what made God real and the object of one's loyalty as well as one's search was His hidden dimension, as much as it was His revealed aspect. "Thou art a God who hides," exclaims the Psalmist. "The hidden things belong to the Lord our God, the revealed things to us and our children," declares the Torah.

Are you puzzled, at times, to the point of despair about such seemingly incongruous blanks in a God-governed world as the death of little children, the birth of misshapen creatures, the pain and agony that invest our human ventures? Then remember that all reality, including the reality of God, stretches far beyond the tiny beam of light that is human reason and understanding.

Why

Organized

Religion?

N O ONE has really crossed the threshold of maturity who has not, somewhere along the road, in his reflections on religion, faced the question: Why does one need any specific time, or mode for the expression of that impulse? Is it not rather artificial to impose form and measure on what should be the spontaneous upsurging of the heart whenever the mood moves us? "I can pray," I have often heard young people say, "when I am walking through the woods, or when I see a majestic sight of nature. Why must I come to the synagogue?"

I over-elaborate the question, but I do so deliberately since I want to take it in full seriousness and meet it head on in its most complete articulation. Similarly, when I use the term, organized religion, I would have you understand by it the whole sweep of religious forms: a synagogue, an order of service, a ritual, specific sacred days, sacred writings, etc.

There are several answers to the question, and each supplements the other. Begin with what is a reasonable assumption and with what is, in fact, implied in the question. Man has a native capacity or potentiality for religious self-expression. Now draw an analogy between that capacity and any one of several other capacities with which man is endowed—let us say, the capacity of speech. What would happen to it, and with it, unless the child heard speech, words and sentences, first from its parents, then from playmates, classmates, teachers, books, etc.

The result is readily imaginable. We learn to speak, though we have all the requisites of speech, only by listening to others. To be sure, once we have acquired fluency and mastery in a language, and we have especial gifts of expression, we begin to express ourselves in a style reflective of our own personality. No matter how distinguished and distinctive the style we create, no one ever creates his own language. The resources of the language at one's disposal remain the indispensable tools, the building blocks for our own self-expression.

The inference is too obvious to be drawn out at any length. Only out of a tradition, only out of and by means of established ways in religion, is religious self-expression possible. The nuances, the inflections, may be ours and, indeed, ought be, but these would be totally impossible without the resources of tradition.

So, then, the first answer to the question, "why organized religion?" parallels the obvious answer to the question, "why grammar or spelling or a literary tradition?" I certainly recognize that the answer is extremely broad and roughly analogous. From the general, and somewhat abstract, then, let us descend to the concrete, and consider the question in one of its specifics.

Why does one need a time and place for prayer? As for the place, let me state at once, that while Judaism recognizes special merit in attendance at the synagogue, it by no means discountenances private prayer at home, or wherever one

18

might be. (Even public prayer, a *minyan,* as you know can be held anywhere.) The attachment of special merit to prayers in the synagogue is, at least in part, a recognition that things that do not have a special time and place somehow get lost in the constant stream of responsibility, distraction and diversion. How much music would there be in the lives of most of us if we did not occasionally go to concerts or sit ourselves down to listen to records, and simultaneously shut out all other matters?

But what of spontaneity? How can it be expected of any-one to be in the mood for prayer on a certain day and at a certain hour? The answer is that no such expectation is made of us, nor is the mood really required. Consider by way of analogy the professional writer for whom writing is part of his daily regimen. I have yet to hear of a writer worth his salt who turned to his desk only when he felt inspired to write. The plain truth is that the genuine writer has certain fixed hours for writing and maintains a fairly rigid schedule. He may feel all written out on any particular day, but, in-spired or not, he will sit himself down at his typewriter. And lo, assuming he has the creative touch, he waits patiently, and ideas begin to flow. A spark is enough to turn over the motor, and once it is warmed up it goes. Prayer, too, may start in low gear, but granting that there is a genuine desire to pray, one picks up fervor as one goes along. The Talmud tells us that the pious people of ancient Jerusalem would not begin their prayers immediately upon entering the synagogue, but would sit quietly and wait for a while before beginning the service.

A variation of the question of fixed time and place is that of fixed specific prayer. Why should not every one find his

19

own expression in prayer? Why be bound by traditional prayers? The truth is that in Judaism one is not limited to the traditional prayers. The prayer book (*siddur*) is actually an anthology that has grown over the ages through the process of accretion. Some have been added, from time to time, others have silently fallen into limbo. The *Lecha Dodee*, for example, was introduced only in the 16th century. On the contrary, write a great, moving prayer and I assure you that more than one synagogue will be eager to welcome it into its liturgy.

Creativity in religion, by all means! Humility, however, compels us to admit that religious genius is as rare as artistic or intellectual genius. For as far into the future as we can see, we will have to return again and again to the classic creations of religion, much as we do in art and literature. A twenty-third Psalm is not written every week.

Let me sum up the whole matter by means of an analogy. The human body possesses both stability and a certain flexibility. The skeletal structure assures the body's stability. Without it, no flexibility would be possible. If the body were completely flexible in all its parts, it would collapse into total inertness. Growth, creativity, spontaneity, are possible on the basis of the fixed and the stable. No human power or capacity ever proved effective or significant in civilization unless it took on some organized form. Why ask the impossible of religion? Would we ask those who struggle to assure peace in the world to dissolve their organizations since man naturally yearns for peace? The question answers itself.

6

"Keep Religion Out Of..."

I MUST apologize for failing to respond to many of you who were so kind as to send me Rosh Hashanah greetings and, most especially, to those who took the time to write at length and describe their first High Holy Days away from home. Need I describe for you the burdens of time and effort that befall a rabbi around the High Holy Days—the height of the American synagogue "season?" But rather than share my burdens, I would much rather share my thoughts and convictions. And the one that occupies me at the moment is indeed intimately related to this phenomenon of crowded synagogues on Rosh Hashanah and Yom Kippur and half empty synagogues the rest of the year.

Can there really be a "season" for Judaism? Is it, in its essential nature, a seasonal activity, appropriate for certain days, or for that matter places, and, aside from then, irrelevant? The question may sound foolish but it is prompted by the fact that in the thinking and activities of most of us, such is the case. Let us look briefly at this attitude.

Take, for example, the slogan: "Keep religion out of politics." On a superficial level, one can readily subscribe to that. In a democracy, a man's religious views should neither qualify him nor disqualify him for office. Nor should one vote for a candidate on the grounds that he is a fellow co-religionist. Nor, properly, should a democratic government show preference for one religious group above another. But on a profounder level, how can religion, earnestly held, fail to deeply affect a man's views on what is good and right, and how men ought to live with each other in society, and how nations ought to relate to one another. Is it, for example, conceivable that religion which preaches the brotherhood of man should have nothing to say on the issue of segregation, or nuclear warfare, or slum clearance, or increased educational opportunities for the young and greater security for the aged? Is it not inconsistent, to say the least, to recognize, on the one hand, that the ideas of democracy have their root, at least in part, in the moral values of the Bible and, on the other hand, insist that politics and religion should be unrelated?

Or take a personal moral issue: sex. Religion has certain views on the nature of man. (Of course, not all religions hold the same view. Judaism and Chrisianity, for example, are worlds apart in their respective conceptions of the sexual aspect of life.) But if these views are seriously held, are they not bound to profoundly influence the sexual ideals we strive to uphold?

In a word, religion sets forth certain ideals for the conduct of life, individual and collective, and is not merely a set of sacred days and rituals. To put religion in a cubby-hole, and seal it off from life, is to make a museum piece of it.

Within Judaism, no one understood this better than did the Chassidim. One of their great teachers once said: "A shoemaker who properly sews the sole of a shoe to its last,

22

draws together the upper and lower worlds." That is to say, any work that is done honestly and sincerely is a contribution to the glory of God and the enhancement of life. Ritual, prayers, synagogue, Sabbath and festivals are meant to re-infuse us with the experience of the holy—the sacredness and awe of God and the sacredness that invests life—our own, and that of others. From that experience, if it be genuine, there should come a new dimension in all our activities and in all our relationships to others, as well as to ourselves. That dimension may be summed up as love, truth and compassion.

Each of these, of course, are large themes, and books have been written about them. At this point, I would make one observation. Ultimately, they derive from our inner being, the region dominated primarily by our total emotional stance. They are not the result of ratiocination, nor are they produced by intellectual exercise. In a word, their root is in that area of our lives from which we address God. "He who says," a Chassidic teacher once declared, "that Torah is one thing and life is another is an idolator."

What is the proof of all this? It is the lives of the great religious figures. In Judaism they range from Abraham to Franz Rosenzweig. Their piety expressed itself in everything they did. In Abraham's case, the way he offered hospitality to strangers, and in Rosenzweig's, the way he met and faced his paralyzing illness. (See Glatzer's book *The Life and Thought of Franz Rosenzweig.*)

Religion that makes no real difference soon becomes a matter of indifference.

Religion:
Crutch
Or
Challenge

7

AN OLD, unforgettable teacher of mine was wont to reiterate in class: "Before you can put the right ideas into people's minds, you've got to get the wrong ideas out of their minds." No notion is both more widespread and fallacious than the idea that religion is essentially an anchor, a refuge; and those who are hostile to religion are sure to add—"a crutch." Anyone who takes so distorted a view of religion simply does not begin to understand what real religion, as represented in the best and noblest aspects of Judaism, is all about.

Judaism, in a sense, begins with Abraham. You recall how the Torah launches its recital of the career of Abraham with: "And the Lord said to Abraham, 'Get thee out of thy land, out of thy birthplace and out of thy father's house unto the land which I will show thee.'" Who dares call this a sop or a crutch! Is it not rather a tremendous, overpowering, unsettling challenge—to uproot one's self, break off precious ties of habit and affection, and go out into the unknown in response to the divine call? More than once, the Torah reports that when the going in the wilderness became tough and precarious, the Israelites bitterly remonstrated with Moses: "Is this not what we had said to thee in Egypt—leave us

24

alone, it is better that we serve Egypt than we die in the desert." The human instinct was all for security and safety, even if it be only the security of slavery. The divine call was for freedom with all its risks and hazards.

One final illustration, though the illustrations might be multiplied a thousand-fold. Again and again, when Moses receives the divine call at the burning bush, he hesitates to accept the mission to enter into a struggle with Pharaoh to liberate Israel from Egypt: "Who am I that I should go to Pharaoh and that I should bring out Israel from Egypt?"—"I am not a man of words."—"Send, whomever Thou wilt send" (but do not send me), etc. The divine call to Moses, and indeed to every man, imposes burdens, difficult soul-testing tasks. It shakes us out of our lethargic inertia and confronts us with trying demands.

The illustrations I have cited are the immemorial symbols of a permanent fact. Real religion is a high challenge to which we respond. It is the challenge to make the most and best of our lives. Who, in all honesty, can say at any point, that he is making the most and best of his life?

What, indeed, does that phrase mean? It means, as I see it, living with courage, love and faith.

By courage, I mean, of course, moral courage—the power to stand up for what one believes is true and right and just in the face of public indifference, derision or hostility. How many of us can truly say that we can do just that without flinching? Does not each of us need those moments of inner communion and the sense of rapport with God, which is prayer, to face the tests of moral courage? The challenge of religion is the challenge of moral courage.

In a recent poll, 90% of the people questioned glibly

responded that they fulfilled the commandment, "Love thy neighbor as thyself." A moment's honest reflection should tell us that it is the most difficult thing in the world. To begin with, so many of us are allergic to ourselves, how can we miss being allergic to other people? Again, loving humanity in the abstract is easy. But the people next door, who strain your patience and try your tolerance—that is another matter. Nor is it a matter of love of people alone. Basically, our attitude toward people reflects our attitude towards life itself. Our boredom, our cynicism, our selfishness, are all telling evidence that our love of life is far from unmixed with strains of bitterness and resentment. So then, to achieve love is an unending challenge—the challenge with which religion confronts us.

Finally, there is the challenge of faith in the Power that stands behind the universe and with whose wisdom and beneficence the world and life are streaked. Faith is an unending quest, the challenge to look at the worst and still believe in the best. For none of us can it ever be a perfect, complete possession to which nothing can be added and nothing subtracted. There are moments when God seems close and real. And there are times when He seems far off and remote. True faith is always a seeking and a questing for a greater understanding and deeper realization. That, too, is religion's challenge.

Of course, there is the kind of religion which is a crutch and hardly anything more. But then, what great and noble thing in the world has not been caricatured? Does one judge literature or art by its imitations and cheap reproductions, or by its authentic masterpieces? To my mind, the question answers itself.

The Function Of Religion

8

YOU MAY have heard, in one or another form, the following interpretation of the function of religion in human life. Primitive man, lacking the technical skill to control nature, found himself at the mercy of the elements. Awed and frightened, he turned to the gods for help in his struggle for survival. *Timor fecit deos*—(fear made the gods). But as man's mastery of nature grew, thanks to the advance of science, man's dependence on the gods (or God) gradually diminished. Today, whatever psychological or emotional values religion may have had in the past, man has grown completely self-reliant. Religion has outlived its usefulness. Or, as Nietzsche put it so dramatically, "God is dead."

There is another side to the coin and it bears careful examination. A convincing case can be made for the position that if advance in technology has apparently brought a diminution of man's need for God, such advance, in our century, seems to go hand in hand with a decline in human relations. Far from solving man's problems of survival and the enhancement of life, technological advance creates situations that threaten man's survival and simultaneously debases the value of the individual.

27

Let me illustrate. I shall optimistically assume that man will never resort to the hydrogen bomb, a gratuitous assumption, of course. But what of refugeeism? (30 million people were compelled to flee from their homes in the last two decades.) What of the suppression of freedom in wide areas of the world? What of a rampant chauvinism and the heightening of national animosities?

Admittedly, all moral attitudes are contingent upon man's personal relationships. Remove the personal element—the face to face encounter between man and man—and moral standards fall precipitately. Who would think of cheating the corner newspaperman? But how many people would refuse to pocket a coin returned by error in a telephone booth? This is a small symbol.

More and more, in modern life, thanks to technological advance, man's relationships with his fellowman are becoming depersonalized. One illustration, *ad hominem*: As colleges grow in size, the relationship between instructor and student grows more and more distant. The student becomes a number, occupying a seat in a lecture hall. The sociologists call this phenomenon the atomization and the depersonalization of the individual.

Clearly, the assumption that the advance of science will solve all man's problems is a naive oversimplification. As technology grows, the human problem in all its ramifications grows more, not less, complex. It is obvious, too, that man needs something more than the mastery of physical nature if there is to be any increment in our life.

It is my conviction that man needs a vital religion. To me, any religion is vital which succeeds in making the individual feel that his life is of value, not because of any intellectual,

28

aesthetic or material achievement on his part, but simply because there is some kind of affinity, despite all the disparities, between himself and God. In biblical language, that idea is expressed in the assertion that man was created in the image of God. The function of religion as the Bible understands it, is not to aid man in mastering the physical world. That sphere is man's task and prerogative. "Have dominion over the world and subdue it," God says to man in Genesis. The sphere of religion is man's relationship to his fellowman and to God. It is the purpose of religion to teach man to master himself, so that, on the one hand, he does not attempt to play at being God, and on the other hand, he comes to revere the life of his fellowman.

These two are indivisible. Sever man's relationship to God and you sever his relationship to his fellowman. Perhaps that is basically why technological advance has been steadily accompanied by deterioration in human relationship. Reverence for God and reverence for man are indivisible. When men believe that "God is dead" then, to quote Dostoyevsky, "everything is permitted," everything including torture of prisoners of war, xenophobia, brutality, lies, etc.

I see no way out of our predicament except a rebirth of vital religion in the hearts of men.

Science

And

Religion

NOTHING, I aver, troubles young people in their exploration of the world of thought so much as the question of the relationship between science and religion. The very first confrontation is likely to come in high school when we discover that biology and geology offer an account of the origins of man and the world that is at wide variance with the accounts we recall from the Bible. Being young, many of us are prone to draw quick conclusions. We conclude, for example, that science must displace religion.

I really hope that you have long ago resolved in your mind that the Bible is in no sense a scientific book. If it were, then like all ancient texts on science, it would have been outdated and been made irrelevant ages ago. Genesis, in its first chapters, is a religious interpretation of the origins of man and the world. In effect, it asserts that the first generation of the universe represents the will of God, that the creative force at work in the world is of God. This, science can neither prove nor disprove.

If I refer to this fairly simple matter at all, it is to nail down the proposition that the scientific and the religious are two, distinct, non-coordinate approaches to human experience.

One is no more inherently in conflict with the other than length is in conflict with breadth. Let me offer an analogy.

Three men go to visit Niagara Falls. One is an artist, the other a musician, and the third an electrical engineer. The first, inspired by the colors playing on the tumultuous mass of water, paints a picture of the falls. The second, responding to the roar and echoes of the water as it rushes over the cataract, writes a symphonic poem entitled, "Niagara." The third, the electrical engineer, calculates the mass, velocity, and force of the water, and estimates how much electrical energy might be generated from it. Who would say that the painting, the musical composition, and the calculation of the engineer, stand in contradiction to each other?

I recognize, of course, that there are those who say that the only reliable avenue to reality is the way of science. This attitude has been properly dubbed scientism. I reject it, categorically, though I am as much aware as the next man, of the enormous benefits science, in its practical application, has brought humanity. Why?

Science is fundamentally based on measurement, that is, on quantity. Now, I maintain that large and significant areas of human experience are simply not subject to quantification. Indeed, quantity as a mode of evaluation is simply irrelevant. Does that simple every day fact require illustration? Then let this one serve: Scores of writers were vastly more prolific than Shakespeare and yet most of them are best forgotten. Or, how do you quantify love or friendship? Or how do you express in terms of quantity, a man's courage, a man's devotion to truth, a man's loyalty to his cause?

It is not alone the fact that so much of what we experience, know and strive for cannot be measured in physical terms.

31

Scientism suffers from another glaring, insuperable lack. It can never establish values for us. It cannot set up criteria as to the desirable or undesirable. When it does, as some of the devotees of scientism occasionally do, it negates its own principle. In other words, it might in a specific area tell us what is, but it can never tell us what ought to be.

This latter statement begs for clarification. Some years ago, a biologist, Kinsey, published a study entitled, *The Sexual Behaviour of the American Male*. From it, many drew the conclusion that the behavior therein described was normal, appropriate, even desirable. This would be tantamount to saying that because a certain percentage of the population has a cold at one time or another during the course of the year, colds are normal, appropriate and desirable.

More recently, a geneticist, Herman Muller, asserted at a scientific congress that it is now possible to breed human beings by means of sperm banks, artificial insemination, etc. (Shades of Aldous Huxley's *Brave New World* and George Orwell's *1984*!) Thus, the professor maintained, undesirable genes could be weeded out, and desirable genes maintained and propagated. Who would determine what was desirable and what was undesirable? On what basis? Incidentally, in a crude way, Hitler tried the same thing when he ordered euthanasia for thousands of physically handicapped and mentally disturbed people.

Let us, now, contrast the scientific approach and the religious approach to the question of the nature of man. Here, two observations are in order. It has been estimated that the chemicals in man's body—the iron, the potassium, the salt, etc.—are worth approximately 94 cents. Who would accept that estimate of the worth of man? Religion, on the other hand, asserts the infinite preciousness of every human life,— even the least of men—because of its faith that "in the image of God, created He man."

Again, does science really reveal the final nature of man? After all the reports are in—biological, physiological, psychological—there is something in man which eludes measurement. The closest we might come is the psychological. But here, as you are no doubt aware, the theories and methods are almost as numerous as the investigators, and there is little agreement among them. At the end of the longest, most painstaking, scientific investigation the nature of man, that which makes man truly human, remains a mystery. Evolution may explain our physical origins; it has nothing to say about our human destiny.

If neither science, nor certainly scientism, can unravel for us the nature of man, neither can they interpret the meaning and purpose of life. Is there a scientific answer to the question: Is man a significant being in the total scheme of things? Astronomically speaking, man is hardly more than a speck of dust. But, then, it is man who is the astronomer. Religion asserts the cosmic significance of man, a statement which science can neither prove nor disprove.

Most of the mischief in the relationship between science and religion is created by scientists who, by reason of their scientific competence, go out of their own realm and deliver judgments on religion and, by the same token, by religionists who make scientific pronouncements on the basis of their religious understanding and knowledge. To me, a scientist's pronouncement on either the truth or value of religion carries no more weight than a movie star's endorsement of a particular make car. I'll take my judgment on automobiles from an automobile mechanic. Of course, I have the same disregard for religionists who pass judgment on the theory of evolution or any other scientific theory for that matter. For my science, I will go to scientists and their writings. For my religion, I will go to men who spend their lives studying the subject.

Judaism— The Fourth Philosophy

THERE are four philosophies of life. All four revolve around one key question. What is the relationship between the world of physical fact and reality, and the intangible realm of the spirit, the axioms of man's faith and morals, the domain of his dreams of freedom, truth and peace? That is the central hub, and around it men group themselves in four contrasting variations, the four basic philosophies of life.

Two of these need not detain us over long for they have but few adherents in our midst. There is the viewpoint that the physical world is an irredeemable vale of sorrows, a dark, narrow passage-way where man has the opportunity to earn promotion to the world of eternal bliss. Between the two realms there stretches an unbridgeable abyss, and one begins only where the other leaves off.

Then there is the philosophy, widely held in India, that both the physical world and man's self are merely illusion. Behind them there is only one permanent reality, the world-spirit. Man should seek to ultimately merge himself in this one true reality.

The third philosophy counts myriads of adherents and it

transcends all the barriers of race, class, nation and even nominal religion. It is the point of view that there is but one realm, not two. What man cannot grasp with his five senses is a figment of the imagination. What cannot be weighed and measured and expressed in terms of size simply does not exist. The real forces in the world are purely physical and all basic satisfactions derive from the gratification of the senses. There is no realm of universal truth or justice. The real problems of life are the material ones. Solve them and men will live happily ever after.

If this philosophy is true, Judaism must be false through and through. For Judaism both worships an invisible God and declares that there is a realm of eternal truth, justice and mercy whose claims, on occasion, must over-ride man's physical appetites. It declares, moreover, that physical power is not the ultimate arbiter in the affairs of men. "Not by might and not by strength but by My Spirit, saith the Lord."

How shall we expose the bottomless falsity of the third philosophy described above? By considering and reflecting on what we know best—our own selves.

I utter the word "I." What do I mean thereby? My physical frame, this flesh and bones, these organs, this bundle of appetites and reflexes? That, I would insist, is only part of me. There is another part. There is the I that can hold my appetites in check, the I that chooses between alternative courses of action, the I that hopes, dreams and anticipates, the I that is stirred by music, exhilarated by beauty, and enkindled by an idea beautifully expressed. There is the I that wants to love and be loved, the I that asks: Who am I? Where am I? and goes off in search for answers.

36

I have lived many years with that self, and yet I have never seen it. No microscope can reveal it. It is as intangible as the wind but as real and close as hands and feet. That real invisible self is attuned, more or less, to an equally invisible and equally real world, the world of the spirit. If that were not so, I could not begin to understand human experience, for wherever I look I see men commanded by ideas and seeking to transform the world by them. What makes a man act beyond the call of duty? What makes an artist pour out his life's strength in his work? What makes us stand up for an unpopular cause, expose ourselves to ridicule and insecurity if there were not some invisible realm making claims on us that override the claims of the actual.

Somehow, it is always the intangibles that give value and meaning to the tangibles, that lift them up and put them on another level. Look at friendship! When I regard my friend simply as a person who can be helpful and useful to me, he is no longer a friend but rather an object to be used. But if between us there is an attitude of trust and confidence, and we readily unburden our hearts to each other, then there is a bond of true friendship. But what are trust and confidence, if not intangible? To this philosophy, which denies both the existence and the value of the realm of the spirit, Judaism opposes its own, the fourth basic philosophy of life. Simply put, it comes down to this: There are two realms—the realm of the physical, the bread and butter realities, and the realm of the spirit, the world of faith and morals, the dreams of the human heart and the world of the divine. Man must ever seek to irradiate the world of the real by the ideal, and ever strive to lift up the former to the level of the latter. That is the task and glory of man. Without the illumination of the spirit, the devotion to ends and values that transcend the physical, life becomes a dark meaningless confusion.

**What
Ought
A
Jew
Believe?**

YOU ASK, is there a test of faith, a series of beliefs to which one must assent if he is to be regarded as an adherent of Judaism?

At no time in the long history of Judaism was there any organized effort by an official representative body of rabbis to draw up a "creed" or a list of dogmas. In the 12th century Maimonides did draw up thirteen principles of belief as basic to Judaism, but despite his enormous authority as a Jewish scholar, he was roundly attacked. By what authority, it was asked, did he declare certain beliefs to be indispensable to Judaism, and others, by implication, merely of secondary importance. I believe that his critics were right and Maimonides was wrong. The critics displayed excellent historical sense. Describing Judaism in the first centuries of the common era, George F. Moore (the late Professor of the History of Religion at Harvard) writes: "This unity and universality (among Jews throughout the world) was not based on Orthodoxy in theology, but upon uniformity of observance." (*Judaism*, Vol. 1, p. 111, Harvard University Press, 1927.)

A belief in God is obviously basic to Judaism, but how

39

are we to conceive of God? Here, Judaism permits an extraordinary latitude. In a famous passage, Maimonides declared
that any Jew who conceives of God in anthropomorphic terms
is an idolator. His critic and commentator Abraham Ibn
Daud sharply comments on the passage as follows: "Greater
and better men than he conceived of God in such terms and
yet they were good Jews." And again Ibn Daud is right. It
is alien to the very nature of Judaism to set up a rigid
series of completely articulated dogmas, belief in which constitutes a test of Judaism. Did not the rabbis of the Talmud
declare that he who denies idolatry is a Jew? Beyond that,
they assert that there are but three *Mitzvot* (commandments)
for which a Jew must be prepared to die (according to one
rabbinic opinion there are but two such *Mitzvot*), rather
than transgress. These are, idolatry, murder and sexual
immorality.

Clearly then, creed plays a role in Judaism quite other
than it does, say, in Christianity. There is no recitation of
a creed in Jewish worship. The closest we ever came to that
was the ancient practice, since abandoned, of reciting the
ten commandments during the service in the Temple in
Jerusalem.

The history of the Jewish beliefs reveals growth and
change. For example, one would look in the Bible in vain
for a belief in reward and punishment in the afterlife,
though in talmudic times this concept comes to the fore
prominently. All divine rewards and punishments in the
Bible are expressed in terms of good and evil in *this* life.
Obviously, this process of clarifying belief is still going on.

As I have indicated, only in the Middle Ages did Jewish
philosophers attempt, with little agreement among them-

selves, to draw up a list of the essential dogmas of Judaism. (It is more than likely that in this effort they were influenced by the contemporary church for whom the exact definition of creed was a matter of the highest moment.)

But a vast and crucial difference existed, and still exists, between the role of dogma in the synagogue and in the church. For the latter, belief in the established creed is a prerequisite both for membership in the church and salvation. While Judaism has its basic beliefs, throughout its history it has decidedly tended to place its emphasis on deed rather than on creed. The Jewish religion is, so to speak, an empirical pragmatic religion. No sheer faith, as such, automatically guarantees anyone salvation, either now, or hereafter. Characteristic of this attitude is the talmudic statement the sages ascribe to God. God says, "Would that Israel forsook Me and observed My Torah, for eventually the light that is in it would bring them back to Me."

It is only in the context of this understanding of the historical place of creed in Judaism that we can confront the contemporary question of our own beliefs and Jewish faith. Here, I would suggest the following considerations which, though general in character, have direct relevance to Judaism: this belief has significance which makes a difference in our lives, that directly or indirectly affects our attitudes and our acts. If it does not, it simply doesn't matter. The ultimate Jewish concern (faith) centered in the past, as it does today, about three things: God, the people of Israel, and Torah.

If these have positive meaning for you, if they elicit from you reverence and trust, a desire to be forever counted among the people of Israel (you as well as your descen-

41

dants), if you feel yourself committed to respond to Torah with an earnest quest to ponder its meaning and appropriate for yourself whatever you can, in all honesty—then this is your Jewish faith. Your concept of God may not tally with mine, your view of the nature of the Jewish people may diverge from mine or from that of other Jews, you may look upon the Torah with different eyes, but that is your prerogative. Neither I, nor any one else can read you out of the Jewish community of faith.

Thus, there is no made-to-order, prefabricated answer to the question, what ought a Jew believe? I rejoice that there is none. All that is required of us is that we relate ourselves, affirmatively, to three central forces: God, Israel and Torah.

How Shall We Conceive Of God?

A STORY will serve as my point of departure for this Letter. The story is told that a mother once noticed her little son busily occupied in drawing a picture. Upon inquiring what kind of picture he was drawing, the startling reply came back: "I am drawing a picture of God." The mother remonstrated, "But, dear, no one knows what God looks like." Undaunted, the child answered, "They will, when I am through."

I promise you no picture of God when I am through. How can I? The prohibition against making images of God is as clear as it is central in Judaism, ancient and modern. But I do have some suggestions on how one can know God without resort to mental images. In this effort, I take my cue from the Bible. On the one hand, it insists repeatedly that "man cannot see God and live," and that, "you saw no image on the day you stood at Sinai." Yet, the Bible does not tire of commanding Israel to "Know God." The prophet speaks of the day when "the earth will be full of the knowledge of God, as the waters that cover the seas." "I will betroth thee unto Me forever and thou shalt know God," declares the Prophet Hosea.

Translated into our terms, the concept might be stated thus: While man can never fathom God ("Thou art a God who hides," declares the Psalmist), man can, and does, have experiences of the living God. Such experiences as give the being of God unshakable certitude. I offer a simple analogy. No one has ever seen an actual atom and yet the existence of the atomic structure and its functioning are inescapable; otherwise there would be no explanation of phenomena that are observed. From the nature of these phenomena the character of the phenomena is deduced.

The experiences that point to the nature of God may be categorized as the experience of order, of change, of dependence, of transcendence and of value. All of them, as we shall presently see, are normal, everyday experiences available to all, though at times, they come to us with heightened force. Let us consider them briefly, in turn.

Order, arrangement, pattern, are ineffaceably stamped on every aspect of our experience of the world, physical and human. Whether it be the waxing or the waning of the seasons, the budding, the flowering and the withering of the tree, or the birth, growth and decay visible in the human world, all things evince a distinctive order. Cause and effect, before and after, constitute an unbroken chain that weaves its way through all experience. Order implies intelligence. (A person who lacked all sense of the relationship between cause and effect would lack all intelligence.) Thus, we can say that God reveals His nature through a universe streaked through and through in its every aspect by order. "How manifold are Thy works, O God," exclaims the Psalmist, "Thou hast made them all with wisdom." An experience of the intelligibility of the world, then, is an experience of God.

"All things change and we with them," declares the Latin proverb. Change, whether in the physical world or in the realm of human affairs, is no illusion. The point need hardly be stressed in an age marked by fantastic inventiveness. The conclusion, however, to be drawn from the fact of change must be noted. This is an open-end universe, inexhaustible in its unimaginable possibilities. Even the past changes, since every age finds new meaning in it and seeks to re-interpret it anew. So, then, whether past or present, the experience of change is omnipresent.

What does the experience mean but that at the heart of all things there abides an infinite creativity, an inexaustible power, to call the new into being. When we experience this process (and who does not?) we experience God at work. Do you recall the opening paragraph of the *Maariv* (evening) Service? "Blessed art Thou, O Lord, God of the universe, who by His word changest the times and variest the seasons."

Dependence is an experience, at least in the human realm, at which we, in our time, are prone to look at askance. Is not the goal of human maturation freedom and independence? True enough, but you must recall that even human independence can emerge only out of dependence. We are born dependent, but if your parents and teachers are wise, they will gradually lead you along the road that leads to independence. Factually speaking, however, there is no absolute independence in the human world no more than there is in the physical world. Even in the full bloom of our maturity we are inter-dependent beings, bound up with one another for weal and woe. That is how the world is made. "No man is an island, each man is part of the continent, what diminishes man, diminishes me." (John Donne) A hundred times a day, we know the experience of dependence: a teacher's knowledge, a friend's love, the beauty of a picture, etc. When I become thoughtfully and gratefully aware that the sources of my being lie beyond myself, when humble gratitude fills my heart for all that I receive, I have an experience of God, of Him who sustains my life. ("And underneath are the everlasting arms.")

Once again: Man is the being who can transcend himself. That is to say, there is nothing that I can achieve, that I can make or fashion, that I cannot imagine a higher achievement, a better method, or a more perfect accomplishment. There is in all of us a drive to excel ourselves. The great thrill of the Olympic Games always is the breaking of previously established records. Always there is the quest, the unending search for a better way, "a more perfect union," a better, more just, social order, a wider expansion of human frontiers. This is what I mean by the experience of transcendence. To know it, is to know God, for God is He who is beyond our grasp and calls us to exceed ourselves. In traditional terms, the concept is found, for example, in the biblical story of Abraham, which opens with the words: "And the Lord said unto Abraham, 'Get thee out of thy land, out of thy birthplace and out of thy father's house unto the land which I will show thee.'" Even there, there will be no final fulfillment of the divine purpose. For the story goes on to declare: "And I will make of thee a great people, and all the families of the earth will be blessed through thee."

Finally, the experience of value. Though the subject is vast I will speak of but one essential aspect. We do not create values. We are grasped by them. Justice commands us, compassion stirs us, truth ordains, beauty invites us irresistibly. In all these there is an element of necessity, compulsion, of which we are aware even if and when we seek to avoid it. That is what I mean when I write that we are grasped by values. That compulsive element is God addressing you and me and calling us to fulfill His will. "What doth the Lord require of thee, O man, but to do justice, love mercy and walk humbly with the Lord, thy God."

There are times when the experiences described above come to us with an overwhelming force. In these moments we have a genuine religious experience and nearness. Besides these, there is another religious experience, that of the holy. The latter, however, is so encompassing that I must perforce reserve the theme for my next Letter.

13

Judaism:

A

Unique

Religion

THOUGH this letter is being written on the Eve of Purim, it will not deal with anti-Semitism. However, it will be based on a statement in the *Megillah,* (Book of Esther), by that archetypal anti-Semite, Haman. Denouncing the Jews to the King, Haman declares: "Their laws are diverse from those of every people."

Now, there are those among us who say that Haman's charge is pure slander. Jews are not different. Hath not a Jew eyes, ears, nose, dimensions? If you prick us, do we not bleed? Much of the current anti-defamation propaganda is based on the desire to refute Haman's assertion, and seeks to prove that Jews are no different from anyone else.

But, if that be so, the inevitable question arises: If there be nothing distinctive about us, why seek to preserve our identity, why do we segregate ourselves as we do for specific Jewish purposes? If between us and the non-Jewish world there are no genuine differences, if Jew be a label without content, why maintain that label?

For all its slanderous intent, Haman's charge is true. Jews are different—though, of course, it is as irrational to resent Jews because they are different as it would be, say, to

48

resent red-headed people because most people are either brunettes or blondes. What are the essential Jewish differentia?

First, the Jew approaches his God directly, never through a mediator. For us, God is revealed through Torah, the ancient record of our people's divinely inspired efforts to pattern their lives, individual and social, in accordance with noble religious and moral ideals. In that record, we find motivation, direction and inspiration to seek the highest possible level of action. Aside from the question of the myth involved in God becoming man (or man becoming God), the Jew does not seek to imitate the life of any man. Imitation is never authentic, and the lack of authenticity is the death knell of genuine religion. Someone once said humorously the reason Jews do not accept Jesus is that it is unthinkable for one Jew to worship another. The life and personality of Jesus, no matter how interpreted, is the central hub of Christianity in all its forms. The Jews approach to God and life is through Torah, as we have defined it.

Again, as much as Judaism is a way of life meant for the individual Jew, it is the way of life of a community, a people. Always, we address God, as Our God and God of our fathers, God of Abraham, Isaac and Jacob. Even in prayer, the most personal and intimate aspect of religion, the Jew approaches God not as an isolated individual, but as a member of a people that has committed itself to strive to be a "Kingdom of priests and a holy nation."

History has made us Jews what we are, just as a man's social environment makes him truly human. True, because of this we have been called clannish and self-segregating. But by the same token, Judaism means, as it has always meant,

49

a profound sense of kinship and responsibility for fellow Jews. The record, past and present, will indicate that this, far from being an ideal to which the Jew pays lip-service, has been a potent factor in Jewish experience. A convert to Judaism not only accepts the people of Israel as his people, but the entire faith of Israel.

Is this ideal in conflict with the ideal of universal loyalty to mankind? No more than my love for my mother is in conflict with my sense of respect and reverence for all mothers. But it is only through the former that I can ever hope to come to the latter. This sense of Judaism as being part of a people with a history, past, present and future is unique to Jews.

Likewise, unique to Jews and Judaism is the conviction that the redemption of man lies ahead of him, not behind him. No event in the Jewish past forms the central climactic event in human history as, say, the appearance and death of Jesus forms the climax of the Christian conception of history. Even Eastern religions, like Buddhism, speak of the reincarnation of Buddha, the repetition on a lesser scale of the original manifestation of Buddha. We Jews say that the Messiah—the dramatic symbol of the redemption of Israel and mankind—is yet to come. (We are not concerned here to argue the point. We intend simply to point out those things that mark the Jew and Judaism as different.)

Christianity, and especially its Protestant version, is essentially a "feeling" religion where the emphasis is on inner emotional states. You have, no doubt, seen the signs: *"Believe* in Jesus and be saved!" Judaism is a religion whose accent is not on feeling, but on doing. Perform the *mitzvot* (the acts of righteousness and piety). Study Torah, says the

Talmud. Even if at first you do not do it for its own sake, eventually you will come to study the Torah for its own sake. Here, psychology reinforces the Jewish attitude. Deeds create emotions, not vice versa. (The James-Lange Theory of Emotions.) But be that as it may, the deeds which Judaism insists upon are not merely the ritual acts ordinarily denominated as religious. Here is a quotation from an old *Mishnah* (the code of Jewish law compiled about the year 200 C.E.): "These are the things of whose fruits a man eats in this world, and the stock thereof remains for the world to come: honoring father and mother, deeds of loving-kindness, attendance at the House of Study, hospitality to wayfarers, visiting the sick, dowering the bride, accompanying the dead to their last resting place, making peace between a man and his neighbor."

This brings us to one final consideration. The customary distinction made in the Western world between the secular and the religious is unknown in Judaism. There is no sphere of life which Judaism does not seek to hallow. The God we worship is not confined to the synagogue. The Psalmist did not say the glory of the Lord fills the Temple. He did say: "The glory of the Lord fills the whole earth." There is, according to Jewish thought, no occasion or situation, no occupation or relationship in which man is involved, which cannot bring to him a sense of the divine. A Chassidic teacher once taught: "A man can make an idol of anything, even of God." We make an idol of God when we restrict Him to an official place of worship.

Enough has been said, we trust, to indicate that Judaism, and hence Jews, are different. William James once remarked that there is not much difference between one man and the

51

next, but what there is, is mighty important. So it is with religious cultures. Only the unthinking and ignorant can keep on parroting the foolish notion that "all religions are basically the same."

What

14

Is

Holy?

IN his memoirs, a French anthropologist relates this interresting story: Travelling once in the Arabian Desert, he was taken captive by a semi-barbarian tribe of Bedouins who, in the primitive way of life, looked upon every stranger as an enemy. The suspicious, hostile tribesmen wanted to kill him. They were restrained, however, by the words of their chief who said, "He is our guest. His life is sacred." The writer concludes the tale with this comment which I paraphrase: "I owe my life to the fact that the sense of the holy still exists among semi-barbarous people."

Does the sense of the holy still exist among modern men? Yes, but its manifestations are vague, faded, and all but washed out by the rationalist, utilitarian spirit that has penetrated virtually every aspect of life in the past two centuries. I count this attribute of man's normal, natural response to the experience of the holy as one of the tragic, all but fatal, maladies of modern civilization. And like all the basic categories of human experience, there is no substitute for it, neither science, art nor technology.

For the holy is as essential a dimension of human experience, as necessary for the wholeness of life (the word wholeness and holiness are related), as the quest of know-

53

ledge or the need of love. So basic is it, that when its normal expression is dammed up, it seeks its object in idols, be they objects, groups, processes, persons or philosophies that are raised to the level of the absolute.

But what is the holy? It is that attitude of awe, reverence and humility which man experiences in the presence of anything which helps him to the transcendent source of his being—God. That "anything" can be a book (the Torah), a place (the synagogue) a day (Yom Kippur), luminous personality, (the *zaddik,* the righteous, holy man), the crucial acts of life (birth, marriage, death).

That is the first aspect of the holy. Always it points beyond itself to the sphere of the ultimate, and while it touches and penetrates the tangible here and now, it extends beyond it infinitely. The holy discloses and reveals God, in so far as the infinite can be revealed and grasped. It points to the divine dimension of life which man can and does experience.

But whatever its object, the place or the process which man regards as holy—the latter is not essentially an inherent quality like magnetism—resides in whatever it is that is regarded as holy. In Judaism, holiness takes on ethical meaning ("The Holy God is sanctified by righteousness") without however losing its meaning as an experience of relationship to God.

Let me illustrate. The holiest ritual object in Judaism is the Scroll of the Torah *(Sefer Torah).* Yet, according to Jewish religious law, a *Sefer Torah* may be sold, if necessary, to ransom someone taken captive. Again, the reiterated command is directed to man, "Ye shall be holy"—"and ye shall sanctify the Sabbath." That is, it is within man's power to endow life and time with sanctity. (Indeed, the chapter

54

in the Torah that opens with the words, "Ye shall be holy for I, the Lord your God, am holy," is regarded by our ancient sages as the chapter which includes the basic principles of Judaism.) It goes without saying that God, too, sanctifies places and time. ("And God hallowed the seventh day and He blessed it.")

Essentially, in Hebrew the word to hallow *(kadesh)* means to set apart, to remove from the sphere of everyday and hence to lift something from that level on which utilitarian considerations predominate. From this consideration, we arrive at two salient aspects of the holy.

The holy is to the commonplace what poetry is to prose. And what is poetry to prose? A more exalted, stirring mode of both experience and expression, something to be approached in a mood altogether different from that which prevails in the everyday. Hence, it is to be approached with awe and humility. As Moses approached the burning bush, he heard the Voice command: "Remove your shoes from off your feet, for the ground on which you stand is holy ground." Let me offer an illustration.

In Judaism, the act of marriage is known as *kiddushin* (sanctification). Even in ordinary speech, we speak of it as an occasion and, of course, invest the ceremony with solemn dignity and formality. What would we think of a marriage ceremony that was carried out in the spirit of casual informality, in which word, gesture and posture were not to be distinguished from those that prevail on the everyday level? Would we not feel that a sacred moment and experience had been desecrated?

One final aspect of the holy. To use it for our own ends, or for profit, is not simply to reduce it to the level of the ordinary, but to profane it. The holy is not opposed to the

55

everyday; it is opposed to the profane. Holy and secular are not contradictory terms any more than left and right are; they are rather complementary, and often enough it is difficult to tell where the boundary between the two runs. Where the boundary line is unmistakably clear, he who treats the holy as something to be exploited for gain, pleasure or prestige, commits the ultimate offense.

I have in mind here not only what is usually denominated as the religious, but no less the realm of deep, personal, intimate human experience. For I insist that there is something of the holy in the human personality. Is it not, according to the teachings of Judaism, stamped in the Divine Image? And yet, what aspect of man's most deeply felt experience is not exploited in our twentieth century for gain, prestige and perverse pleasure? Indeed, the publication with pictures, and the description of the profoundest personal experiences of prominent people, is a regular feature of much of our press and periodicals. It is only one step from nothing private to nothing sacred.

As you reflect on these things, I trust you begin to see how the process of the desacralization of life leads to a cheapening, a vulgarization and a degradation of life and to boredom. If all hours are like all other hours, and thus there are no sacred moments; if all places are alike, and there are no sacred places and no sacred objects; if man lives in homogenized space and time, then he is indeed living in a wasteland. For myself, I trace the flattening out of so much of modern life, the quality of boredom that suffuses so much of it, the loss of genuine value, all these, and similar phenomena, to man's tragic loss of the sense of the sacred.

But what was it the old Latin proverb asserted?—"Drive nature out with a pitchfork, nevertheless it will return."

56

Modern man's sense of the holy has returned in the form of the idolization of the state, of money, of much publicized personalities (consider the homage and awe with which the multitude regards movie stars). Most tragic of all in its consequence is, of course, the desacralization of man himself. And, hence, I return to the episode with which I began this letter. Out of the sense of the holy there has come man's sensitivity. Where that root is cut and permitted to languish, how long will it take before moral consciousness withers?

*On
Being
At
Home
In
The
Synagogue*

I WANT to discuss and analyze with you a problem presented to me recently by a college student. While it is far from universal, it raises issues and considerations that should be of concern and interest to all of us.

This student attended Friday evening services on campus and found them disappointingly dull and uninspiring. Since his particular school requires a certain amount of compulsory chapel attendance, the student has taken to attending Christian services, drawn as much by curiosity as by the necessity to comply with college regulations. While he found a number of things in the service that stuck in his throat, and in which he could not join, he found many of the prayers and hymns inspiring and engendering a genuine religious mood. At the same time, he feels that he is violating his Jewish conscience, and the whole business of attending Christian services produces in him, we suspect, a sense of guilt. But, on the other hand, what is one to do if the particular Jewish service available leaves one untouched and unmoved? That is the problem.

To resolve this problem honestly and thoughtfully, the

approach must be by way of several general, preliminary, but necessary, observations. Meaningful prayer, that truly engages the heart and the spirit, must perforce be entered into without intellectual or emotional reservations. *Au fond,* prayer is one expression of our feeling of being at home in the world, and our unforced striving to seek a deeper rapport with man and God. There can no more be mental and emotional reservations in praying than there can be in authentic love. In love, we respond completely to the total person. The imperfections of the person—imperfections of beauty or character—though we may objectively be aware of them, do *not* erect barriers between us. Two people truly in love either accept each other completely as they are, or they do not.

A religious service, in which one cannot conscientiously join because of its central features and affirmations, cannot be one in which we are truly part of the congregation. Need we enumerate the features of a Christian service, even of the liberal variety, which make unqualified participation on the part of a Jew impossible?

Those that do not meet the eye deserve consideration. The very day (Sunday) on which Christian services are held, constitutes an affirmation in which no Jew can join unless, of course, he has already abandoned Judaism in favor of Christianity. Sunday is not simply the Christian Sabbath. It is the "Lord's Day"—the day on which Jesus, according to Christian faith, rose from the dead. It is, however construed and interpreted, the Christian's testimony to his faith in the supernatural character of Jesus.

The barriers we speak of are not alone those which must necessarily stand between a Jew and certain elements in the Christian service: the ritual, the day, etc. There are others no less impermeable.

59

Worship in a house of prayer is not a solitary act, it is essentially communal in nature. In a synagogue, church or mosque, one is part of a congregation, a group of people bound together by common commitments and affirmations. In the case of Jews, one adds common history and a group of symbols that express the history and the faith that made it what it is.

Jewish prayer is essentially the congregation of Israel in prayer. Though the God we worship is the universal God— and the universality of God (monotheism) is Judaism's first, if not sole, distinguishing characteristic—yet, we Jews speak of God quite often as "the God of Abraham, Isaac and Jacob," as "The Rock and Redeemer of Israel," etc. That is to say, the position from which the Jew approaches God in prayer or thought, no matter what his personal conception of God, is the context of a covenanted people. There is no more private religion than there is a private language. How we use that language, with what skill and command, depends, of course, upon our own individual powers. The native tongue of the Jew is Judaism. Are not Moses, Jeremiah, the Psalmist, Hillel, Akiba, Maimonides, all the way down to Buber and Rosenzweig, sufficient indication that in devoted, skillful hands it is a most exquisite instrument worthy of the most gifted of us?

All of which brings us to our final and practical consideration. A poor rendition of a Friday evening service—and God knows I have, alas, witnessed many such—is no more evidence of Judaism's religious poverty than an execrable, blundering performance of Beethoven's Ninth is proof of Beethoven's inadequacy as a composer.

Then, what is to be done in the circumstances described by the student? (Since I am obviously not informed on all the details of the service, what it consists of, etc., I am only able to conjecture when I make the following suggestion): Go and speak to the person in charge, honestly and constructively. Suggest changes in both content and style: perhaps the use of a different *Siddur;* some explanation of the prayers; some beautiful inspirational readings from Jewish literature.

The Sabbath is the glory of Judaism. If a particular Friday evening service fails to convey its spirit, then it is the fault of the performers, not the score. As a mere indication of what Sabbath prayer, song, hymn and poetry mean to one sensitive contemporary spirit, I append a brief poem. Heine wrote of "Die Prinzessen Shabat" (The Sabbath Princess): "Even shabby nondescript garments, cannot utterly conceal her intrinsic beauty and spiritual meaning." If anyone has a contribution to make, by way of adding to the adornment of the Sabbath bride and making her weekly visit the inspiring thing it should be, by all means, let him make it. He or she will have the satisfaction of knowing that they stand in a long line of great spirits that began with the writers of the Bible down to the poets and thinkers of present day Israel. At-homeness is the heart of religion. In Judaism, the Jew is at home. Elsewhere, he must forever be a stranger.

16

The
Troubles
Of
The
Atheist

IT IS commonly presumed that the religionist, the man who believes in God, has a lot of explaining to do, while the atheist, refusing to give credence to God, has no problems. It seems to me that the very contrary is true. To be sure, as we shall presently see, the religionist reaches a point where all he can do is to repeat after Job: "Canst thou, by search-ing, find out God?" But consider the case of the atheist and the enormous riddles he faces, or rather, refuses to face.

First, there are the unmistakable signs of purposiveness built into the very structure and operation of the universe. He must explain why there is a cosmos at all. (Even if it were all chaos, he would have to offer an explanation why there was something rather than nothing.) Why does the physical world hang together and why is it related, like an organism in all its parts? The merest blade of grass reflects the sun millions of miles away, the oceans, the earth, etc. Again, why the evolutionary thrust that brings forth ever higher forms of life?

Again, if all is accidental, a purposeless collocation of atoms, how explain the emergence of spirit? By the latter, I mean something quite concrete: the values of truth, beauty and goodness; values so precious that again and again men

62

will forego material advantage for the sake of these spiritual values.

Even more! How explain the creativity that marks both the physical universe and human civilization? How explain man's power of self-transcendence, the power to direct one's action in the light of goals not yet realized.

Clearly, the questions to be answered on the theoretical level might be indefinitely increased, and many will readily suggest themselves.

But man does not live by thought alone, even as he does not live by bread alone. If, ultimately, what one cherishes most from the atheistic view point is at the mercy of meaningless chance and, hence, doomed to begin with, where does one find the morale to keep going in the face of adversity and defeat? The Psalmist could say, "I lift up mine eyes unto the mountains, whence cometh my help. My help cometh from the Lord, the Maker of heaven and earth." Where can the atheist lift up his eyes to? Unlike Job, his bleak philosophy will not even afford him the small comfort of cursing the day he was born. (Since the atheist cannot bless, he cannot curse.)

Finally, if at the heart of things there is meaninglessness, and pure inexplicable chance is king (a concept impossible to grasp), on what does one build a set of moral standards? "The greatest good to the greatest number?" On that principle, a slave-holding society could hardly justify its existence, since there were more freemen than slaves. On what shall we base the dignity of the individual? On the basis of an atheist philosophy, does not man become nothing more than an object, and hence to be treated as such?

So, the difficulties of the atheist pile up and his position reminds one of the reported conversation of two boys who had just read a bit about astronomy, and discovered that the blue sky was really an optical illusion. "There ain't no blue sky," said one. "Why," replied the other, "what is there, then, that ain't?"

Compared to all these, the religionist's position is simplicity itself. Not that he's exempt from all problems. On the contrary, he does face the question of disorder and apparent breaks in the scheme of purposiveness in the world. Even after the mind has gone as far as it can — and some appreciable dent on the problem can be made—still, having posited a God, "Whose thoughts are not our thoughts and Whose ways are not our ways," he can live with the mystery. He can live with it, because the mysterious is a category of normal human experience. Who, for example, has ever really explained the mystery of time, or the mystery of the human self?

Actually, the average self-professing atheist lives and acts on a faith he refuses to acknowledge. He manifests morale and moral indignation, as if the nature of things truly justified these. Let me put it this way: The average atheist is a man who lives beyond his philosophic means. The average religionist refuses to live up to his means. If he did, he would find his religion a source of strength and moral life that would move him to joyous deeds of doing rectitude. The atheist would, upon candidly examining his position, either have to live as an atheist should—what's more natural than a meaningless life in a meaningless universe—or else abandon his atheism.

Is A Jewish Way Of Life Possible On Campus?

ONE OF my young friends poses a real problem in a recent letter: "How can a Jewish college student, away from his home and community environment, follow the Jewish tradition amid the circumstances, social and psychological, of the college campus?" This question, I am sure, in one or another of its aspects, if not in its broad formulations, must have troubled all of you. While I have no pat or easy solution, I do have several concrete suggestions, which, if followed, ought give one the sense that one is doing the very best he or she can, under the circumstances.

Broadly conceived, the Jewish tradition consists of three indispensable and basically interrelated aspects. In everyone's Jewish life, it should be possible, even if difficult, to include at least some of the elements of each aspect.

To live within the Jewish tradition, in the first instance, means to live with a sensitiveness to right and wrong. The first question the traditional Jew asks himself is not: Is it fun? or Can I get away with it? but, Is it right? Reduced

65

to particulars, this would mean, Is it right to plagiarize—
To cheat on examinations—To regard other people simply as
instruments for the gratification of one's own desires? Is it
right to look down with contempt on those of lesser attain-
ments than ourselves?

Part of the moral tradition is a sense of communal respon-
sibility. I think it is a fair observation that the average
Jewish college student spends more on a date than his grand-
father earned in a week. There is no moral life without an
element of self-denial. I think every college student ought
to make a regular contribution to a worthy Jewish cause.
The needs of our people abroad, most particularly in
Israel, are simply enormous. I wonder what percentage of
Jewish college students, for example, contribute to the
U.J.A.?

There is no problem or situation in life which does not
contain its moral aspect. A Jew living in the tradition will
weigh the values involved in any situation, and seek the
highest fulfillment.

The second aspect of the tradition is a commitment to
increase our understanding and appreciation of it. This means
to study. Of course, I understand that your obligation to
your own course of study must take priority. And yet, somewhere in your crowded schedule it should be possible to
spend an hour a week reading a good Jewish book, or one
of the classics of Jewish literature, or join a group for an
instructive discussion of some Jewish theme.

Finally, there is, of course, a pattern of Jewish observance.
This includes synagogue attendance, observance of holidays,
dietary laws, etc. These present a particularly acute problem.
While I cannot go into details in a letter, I think the rule
ought to be, do everything that is possible and just a little

more. I grant that an element of sacrifice is involved, whether it be the sacrifice of time or convenience. But loyalty that costs us nothing is not loyalty. That is the acid test. Attending services at the synagogue, or going some distance where it is not in easy reach, is an expression of loyalty to Judaism.

There are two more aspects of the matter. To follow a pattern of Jewish observance in a non-Jewish environment, one runs the risk of being regarded as something of an odd-ball by non-Jews, and, even by some Jews. One must simply have the fortitude, say, to light Chanukah candles even though a non-Jewish room-mate has put a Christmas wreath on the door. In the long run, such earnestness in religious observance gains one respect, not disdain.

Finally, do not take the all-or-nothing attitude towards religious observance. If, for example, one simply cannot observe the dietary laws completely, one should not dispense with them altogether. The abstention from pork products and forbidden sea food can serve as an expression of your commitment to them. In no aspect of life do reasonable people take the attitude of all or nothing. If I cannot have the most exquisite food in the world, would I refuse to eat? If I cannot get a hundred on every test I take, should I abandon the pursuit of an education?

Thus, it appears to me that granted sufficient commitment and strength of character on the part of the Jewish college student, a pattern of a Jewish way of life can be worked out on virtually any campus. And by a Jewish way of life, I mean the three classic elements on which, according to the *Ethics of The Fathers,* the world rests: *Torah* (Jewish study), *Avodah,* (the worship of God and ritual observance), and *Gemilut Chassadim* (the doing of deeds of lovingkind-

67

ness). A life that contains something of each of these is a Jewish way of life.

This, in sketchy outline, is a program for living within the tradition, even in a non-Jewish environment. I know that there are many difficulties involved, but the old rule that it is not easy to be a Jew, still applies. Then again, there is nothing really worthwhile in life that is easy.

18

Does Ritual Make Sense?

I BEGIN this letter with an actual question, posed to me in writing, by a college student. "How important is the complicated ritualistic structure which Judaism has erected? Isn't the ultimate idea to live a good life? Whence *kashrut,* the *Shabbat,* the prayers and services, not to mention the specific rituals surrounding the holidays? I realize that many of the rituals fulfill voids in man, but music or any other art form could easily replace prayer and services."

The present reply will not attempt to analyze any particular set of Jewish rituals. (Some of the more prominent, such as *kashrut,* will be dealt with, *in extenso,* in another letter.) It will, however, seek to present an affirmative attitude towards Jewish ritual based on an analysis of the nature, function and meaning of religious ritual.

In all human experience, that which we cannot express in conceptual terms, because of its abstract nature, we perforce must refer to through symbols, acts, gestures or objects which point to whatever it is we desire to express. There is no area of life in which this does not hold true. A salute to a flag is a symbolic gesture of our loyalty to our country. A handshake is a symbolic expression of friendship. A marriage ring is the symbol of the pledge of love and loyalty. Rising in someone's presence is a symbol of deference and respect. Every day of our lives, each of us performs a score or more of symbolic acts, and we respond to a variety of symbols. Who, on this level, would question the inevitable necessity of symbols to express attitudes, feelings and ideas? Their necessity derives from their power to express these more effectively and cogently than any purely verbal statement. In deed, these very acts, gestures and objects, if they are genuine symbols, bestir in us the very attitudes and feelings they are meant to express. A warm, vigorous handclasp, an embrace, can be more eloquent and expressive of my friendship and fondness for you than the words, "you are my friend." At the same time, the physical act of extending my hand and grasping yours bestirs, and sets in motion, the otherwise quiescent feeling of friendship that I harbor for you.

What do Jewish rituals (symbols) express? They express the sphere of the holy—that dimension of life that, while available here and now, infinitely transcends it. The rituals say that there is more to life than simply objects and acts of common sense. There are some objects and acts through which man can experience that transcendent immanent realm in a way no other avenue offers. The crucial experiences of life, those which mark and make our destiny, are particularly susceptible to becoming infused with the holy.

Hence, in all religions, and of course in Judaism, the crises that mark our passage from one stage of life to another are surrounded by various rituals. (I hasten to add that, as we shall presently see, Jewish religious ritual has its own particular character and meaning.) I offer here but a single illustration. The Jewish mariage ceremony is called *kid-dushin* (literally, sanctification). What does the marriage ritual: the standing together under a canopy, the marriage ring, the sipping of wine by bride and groom from the same cup, the recitation of the *berachot,* the reading of the *ketubah*—what does all this signify and express most eloquently and powerfully? It says to us that a unique relationship is being established between two people, and since it involves all that they have and are, it bears the stamp of holiness. Either marriage is that, or it is simply a convenient housekeeping arrangement, a way of serving the satisfaction of some mutual needs with no more sacred quality than any arrangement people enter into for some mutual benefit. More than once in my experience in the rabbinate, a young couple, though married civilly, in the prosaic, matter of fact manner peculiar to court clerks, has come to me for a religious ceremony. "Somehow," they say, "we don't feel married," even though, of course, they have been living together as husband and wife. In their own way, they were expressing the truth that without religious ritual, which invests our major life experiences with the sense of the sacred, life loses its meaning and glow.

A religious ritual, moreover, participates in that to which it points, and itself becomes invested with sacred character. Again, let me propose but a single illustration. Looked at objectively, a *Sefer Torah* is no more than a scroll of parchment on which the five books of the Torah have been written by hand by a scribe. But because a Torah points to God as the source of its inspiration, we regard it as sacred. We handle it with the utmost deference. We stand in its presence. We do not touch it with our bare hands. We keep it covered

71

when it is not being read, and we guard it in the *Aron Kodesh* (the Holy Ark). Clearly, what gives it its sacred character is not its intrinsic material nature or value but, rather, that with which it is associated. This sacred value and character by association is a universal tendency even in this age when the sense of the sacred appears to be vanishing. The original of the Declaration of Independence is zealously guarded in Independence Hall. Objectively speaking, all it consists of is a few sheets of paper with some writing that has been reproduced millions of times and is available practically for the asking.

Here, we have come upon another important aspect of the function of ritual. It helps recreate for us, as nothing else can, the original context out of which it emerged. When I look at the original of the Declaration of Independence I see again, in my mind's eye, the men and the circumstances that surrounded that document. In a way, I relive that experience.

Think now of the Passover *Seder* and its ritual. Ask yourself, which makes the experience of the Exodus from Egypt more vivid, more real?—tasting the *matzah*, eating the *maror*, seeing the roasted shank bone and egg, or simply reading an account of the departure from Egypt in the 12th chapter of Exodus? Much of Jewish ritual, especially that which surrounds the various festivals, is aimed at a reliving in every generation of the decisive historic experiences of our people in the ancient past. To recall and to re-enact the past, in symbolic dramatic form, is to vibrate in our minds and hearts some of the major cords that go to make up our sense of Jewish identity, our common history. A person whose past simply vanished from his consciousness would lose his sense of identity. A man who cannot remember who he was, what his association with persons, things and places were, simply doesn't know who he is.

Thus, Jewish religious ritual brings us in touch with the sacred and the historical, essential dimensions of what it means to be a Jew. It is not, as my questioner seems to infer, merely an experience in the realm of the aesthetic, and for which any aesthetic experience can readily substitute. When ritual objects lose their sacred character, this can, and does, happen. They then become merely aesthetic objects, providing of course that they have aesthetic character. I can listen to Bach's Mass in B Minor and enjoy it merely as gorgeous music. But to the professing Christian its aesthetic significance is fairly incidental to its religious meaning, though, to be sure, it helps to convey that meaning.

One more word, though the subject is far from exhausted. Religious rituals are, so to speak, the private language of a community of faith. They convey little if anything to those who do not belong. Hence, one set of rituals cannot be substituted for another. A wafer in Christian ritual means one thing, a *matzah* in Jewish ritual means something else altogether.

In all this, I have yet to indicate the very strong and organic tie in Judaism that binds the ritual to the ethical. This I propose to do in my next letter. I began with a question: let me conclude with one. Can man's ethical sense long survive a life stripped bare of the ritual experience?

19

The Ritual And The Ethical

IT IS a commonplace of most versions of Reform Judaism, though its ultimate source is liberal Protestant Christianity, that Judaism's highest expression is in the domain of the ethical—a domain, thanks to the Hebrew prophets, that supplanted the element of ritual. The main thrust of the prophets, so it is claimed, was directed against the ritual practices that clustered around the Temple and its sacrificial service. Their teaching was that the religious demand could only be met by justice, compassion and lovingkindness, not by ritual and sacrifice. To support and buttress this position, many biblical passages are cited. This historical interpretation aside, there is here implied that the ethical and the ritual are in intrinsic opposition, and that, of course, the heart of Judaism is the ethical sphere.

It can be demonstrated as, indeed, it has been by a variety of Jewish scholars, that this historical interpretation is utterly false. The prophets could no more conceive of a religion without ritual than they could conceive of a religion without God. Did they not foresee, in the Messianic days, a rebuilt Temple in which sacrifices would be brought and to which the people would stream? What the prophets did thunder against was the cutting off of the ritual from the ethical, and the exaltation of the former as the sole religious demand. That is to say, they would not tolerate the concept that a mechanical performance of the ritual was an end in itself, and that thereby a man fulfilled his religious duty.

Now, I readily grant that there are those who in our own time look upon Jewish ritual in precisely that way—namely, as an end in itself with no relation whatever to the ethical aspect of life. That, I maintain, is a perversion of authentic Judaism, something in contravention of its profoundest and now essential teaching. Anything, including Judaism, deserves to be judged by its truest exponents, not its worst. (Would we condemn medicine because of the quacks that may be found in the profession?)

But what is the relationship between the ritual and the ethical in Judaism? You will recall, from my previous letter, that ritual's first function is to generate and sustain in man the sense of the holy. It takes ordinary objects and acts, and invests them with sacredness. Specifically, in our context, certain life experiences, as we have seen, are endowed with this character: birth, marriage, death. Thus, man too is susceptible to holiness and must be regarded and treated as inviolable. To treat man as one would any ordinary object, is to be guilty of a violation of the holy (sacrilege).

I believe it can be demonstrated on purely anthropological grounds that man's ethical sense originally arose out of the more primary sense of the holy. However rude and crude ancient man's expression of ethical ideas and feelings, these stemmed, in their origins, out of the taboos which surrounded holy objects including man himself. In our time, we speak of the dignity of the individual. Behind that term, there lurks the notion that a man should not be treated as a tool, valuable only in utilitarian terms; that there is something about him, no matter what his status, which we dare not trample upon for our own purpose, profit or pleasure.

All that I have attempted to express here is to be found in concrete terms in the 19th chapter of the Book of Leviticus, the chapter the rabbis of the Talmud described as the very pith and marrow of the Torah. The chapter opens with the words: "Ye shall be holy for I the Lord your God am holy." It includes the golden rule: "Thou shalt love thy neighbor as thyself," and revealingly enough, cheek by jowl with this moral command, a number of ritual commands. In the view of the Torah, then, there is an intimate positive correlation between the ethical and the ritual. Reverence for life (the phrase is Albert Schweitzer's), is engendered by the experience of sanctifying life's processes and activities. If there be no realm of the holy anywhere (and things must be regarded with awe and reverence but never as an object), how can there suddenly come into being a reverence for life? God and man are in the same co-ordinate: "Ye shall be holy, for I the Lord your God am holy."

The great achievement of the prophets was to establish the ethical dimension as supreme in Judaism. "The holy God is sanctified by righteousness," declares the Prophet Isaiah. Though there is no inherent antagonism between the two dimensions, such however are life's unforeseen complexities that on occasion the two do conflict. Then, of course, Judaism's answer is that the ethical must take precedence. Thus, there is no ritual command that ought not be disregarded in order to save a life. But to argue from this that the ritual is unimportant or even in general opposition to the moral command, is to be guilty of a non-sequitur. I may sometimes have to make a choice between reading a book or visiting a sick friend. Yet, obviously, the two are not inherently opposed to each other nor is the former unimportant. In fact, it may make me a more interesting visitor.

The really great Jewish spirits were those men, and they were innumerable, for whom the ritual and ethical aspects of Judaism formed a single, integrated whole, one reinforcing the other.

**Do
The
Jewish
Dietary
Laws
Make
Religious
Sense?**

20

THROUGHOUT these letters I have sought to make explicit a single, fundamental proposition. It is the understanding that Judaism is essentially a total way of life, that there is no human concern or activity that falls beyond the purview of the Jewish religious tradition. Some have therefore defined Judaism as the evolving religious civilization of the Jewish people. If that is true, then the distinction ordinarily made between religious and secular activities is inapplicable to Judaism. There is, in Martin Buber's phrase, only the hallowed, and that which is not yet hallowed. In the light of this, one understands why so much of Jewish religious living takes place, not in the confines of the synagogue, but in the home and the market place. "You shall have just weights and measures," is as much a part of Judaism as, "Remember the Sabbath day to keep it holy." He who would reduce Judaism to a religion, in the ordinary sense of the word—to prayer and ritual enacted in a specific sacred place—distorts its very nature.

This introduction anticipates the question, what has religion to do with the kind of food one eats? The answer is that Jewish religion is involved in all one does, even in those acts which modern man regards as basically purely physiological. It rejects the Pauline idea that what comes out of a man's mouth makes him pure or impure, not what enters his mouth. Would we not, in our society, regard someone who ate the flesh of a dog or cat as a person who thereby degraded himself to the level of an animal? Do we not call someone who stuffs himself, without limit or restraint, a pig? Do we not respond with disgust when we read that at ancient Roman patrician banquets, the participants regularly overate to such an extent that they normally followed such bouts with an emetic? Clearly, the how and what of our eating do elicit from us strong emotional reaction.

It is a mark of civilization to surround the process of eating with a variety of practices meant to reflect refinement, esthetic sensibility, and the social character of man. If then, the ingestion of food can be, as it is in civilized society, the occasion for the expression of man's social and esthetic sensibilities why cannot it be the occasion for the manifestation of man's spiritual sensibilities? The sages of the Talmud said as much when they declared: "A man's table is his altar."

But before we can enter into any direct consideration of the traditional Jewish dietary laws, at least one widely held contemporary notion on the subject must be shown to be totally erroneous. It, perhaps more than anything else, is responsible for the wide lack of observance of the dietary laws characteristic of modern Jews. It is the notion that the dietary laws were originally intended as measures of preventative hygiene. More times than I can count, I have heard young people say, when discussing· the subject, these laws were necessary in ancient times because they had no refrigeration, no government inspection of meat, etc. Nothing could be further from the truth. The word *kosher* does not mean hygienically clean, but rather ritually fit or proper. The division of the animals in the Torah into the two categories of pure and impure (*tahor* and *tamey*) is certainly not based on any inherent characteristic of the animals, or their eating habits. The chicken is surely no more finicky or refined in this matter than the pig. Thus, we might go on and indicate that this interpretation of the original purpose of the dietary laws can find no essential support in the original laws of the Torah from which the practice of *kashrut* derives. Only later, in the rabbinic period, did this element of hygiene enter so that an animal, though intrinsically *kosher* would basically be declared *treyfah* because of some organic injury. Such instances are occasional, and could not therefore have possibly been the ground for dividing animals, fowl and fish into the two classes, of the permissible and non-permissible. Whatever your attitude to the dietary laws or towards anything else for that matter, it ought not be based on ideas that are demonstrably false.

The real story of the dietary laws begins in the 29th verse of the first chapter of Genesis. God says to the man and woman He has created: "Behold, I have given you all vegetation yielding seed, which is upon the face of the earth, and every tree, bearing fruit yielding seed, shall be for you for food." That is to say that, originally, man was intended to be vegetarian. For in the Garden of Eden, before man lost his innocence, he lived in peace with the animals. To be carnivorous, he would have had to hunt and destroy the animals, and thus become their enemy. This

80

original harmony with the animal world, according to the Bible, is the ideal state which the weakness and folly of man could not sustain. However, in the end of days, man will regain this ideal state.

Permission to eat animal flesh, granted to Noah, is a concession to man's present weakness. Even this concession, however, is not a blanket one. Certain limitations to it are laid down. The blood of the animal which is its life, is not to be eaten (Genesis 9:4). This refraining from eating the blood of the animal (its very life) is a symbolic act, and a reminder that taking the life of any living creature, even that of an animal, is an immoral act. Elsewhere in the Bible, there are indications that the desire for animal flesh is regarded as a kind of lust which, hopefully, man will some day overcome.

From our own perspective, I must say that the moral argument of the vegetarian is really unanswerable and has good biblical warrant. If his position is based on moral grounds, all of us must be humbled by the vegetarian. While few of us are vegetarians, the biblical attitude towards eating the flesh of living things has had a deep impact on the traditional Jewish view of taking animal life. If nothing else, the dietary laws, calling for a specific mode of ritual slaughter, guaranteed among Jews an intense reluctance towards random animal slaughter. The notion of tracking down an animal and destroying it for the sake of sport was revolting, the very acme of cruelty. (In an illuminated medieval Passover Haggadah, reprinted innumerable times, the wicked son is pictured as a hunter.) The dietary laws gave Jews, and still do for those Jews who observe them, an extraordinary aversion to blood, even animal blood. Through the long centuries of Jewish history, it has been observed, no Jewish child ever saw its mother casually kill a chicken with an axe.

But we are running ahead of the story of the dietary laws. Their purpose is clearly stated in the Torah. "And ye shall sanctify yourselves, and ye shall be holy, for I God am holy." (Leviticus 11:44) "For ye are a holy people unto the Lord your God . . . ye shall eat no abomination." (Deuteronomy 12:2,3) To refrain from eating of the flesh of certain animals, fowl and fish, is regarded as a sign of holiness. To eat of them is to defile oneself.

Now you ask, of course, what makes certain animals an "abomination" for the Israelite? (It must be noted, in passing, that the dietary laws were never regarded in Judaism as possessing universal validity for all men. On the contrary, they are directed in the Torah to Israel alone.) Here, the only answer is that every society regards certain animals as unfit for human consumption—taboo, if you will. The reasons probably lie deep in the early history of a particular society, and need not concern us here. But whatever the forbidden animal might be—the cow, for example, among Hindus—to eat of it is to lose something of one's status in that particular society. If, as is the case in Judaism, that society regards itself as a society based on holiness, then to eat of the "abomination" is to defile oneself.

Of all the forbidden animals, it was the pig, due to historical circumstances, that came to be regarded as the most offensive. (The pig was a favorite pagan sacrifice.) During the Maccabean period, the offering of a pig on a pagan altar, and the eating of its flesh, was the sign of a Jew's foresaking Judaism, a manifest demonstration of apostasy.

There is one more aspect of the matter that, even in this

82

brief discussion of the dietary laws, cannot go unobserved. These laws provide for a certain mode of ritual slaughter. The purpose is two-fold. One, that an absolute minimum of pain be caused to the animal in the process of slaughtering it. Thus, an animal that is hacked to death is *treyfah*. Secondly, the slaughtering of the animal is done by a *shochet*, a pious man for whom the act is a ritual, not a mechanical putting to death of an animal.

I trust that though I have not touched on many significant details, the basic picture emerges. *Kashrut* is the Jewish mode of sanctifying one of the basic physical processes whereby human life is sustained. Life must be sustained, but in such a way as to add to the sense of its holiness, not diminish it. The physiological aspects of human life can be occasions for experiencing the holy—that blend of the surpassing significance of existence and the ethical, to which our people was pledged at its very origin, and to which many of us are still pledged.

I don't know whether I have persuaded you to the observance of *kashrut*, but I do hope that at the very least, you now see the laws in a new, and more understanding light.

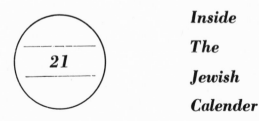

Inside

The

Jewish

Calender

NOTHING, it has been truly said, reveals the nature of Judaism better than the Jewish calendar. Our calendar is marked by the weekly Sabbath and the festivals. If we understand these, we understand a great deal about Judaism. Let us take the festivals first.

In their pre-Israelite origin, these were purely agricultural in nature and celebrated the significant events in the life of the ancient farmer—the coming of spring, the spring harvest and the fall harvest. Judaism took these nature festivals and turned them into historical festivals—occasions that recalled and commemorated the significant historic experiences of our people in the early stages of its existence. History took the place of nature. Though traces of their agricultural character still remain, *Pesah,* in Jewish consciousness is the remembrance of the exodus from Egypt; *Shavuot,* is the time of the giving of the Torah; and *Sukkot,* recalls the years of wandering in the wilderness.

Something not too dissimilar took place in regard to the Sabbath. In pre-Israelite times, probably among the Babylonians, there were certain (four or five) days in the month that were regarded as unlucky, as days on which no business ought be transacted. In Babylonian astrology they were related to various phases of the moon. In Judaism, the Sabbath lost both its connection with phases of the moon and its character as an unlucky day. Instead, it received both a new sanction and a new purpose. In one version of the Ten Commandments, the Sabbath is declared to be the remembrance of the work of creation. It thus receives a cosmic character. In the other version, the Sabbath commandment reads: ". . . in order that your manservant and maidservant might rest like you. And thou shalt remember that thou wast a slave in the land of Egypt . . . therefore doth the Lord thy God command thee to observe the Sabbath day." Here, the sanction and purpose of the Sabbath are historical and social.

What is the meaning of this wresting of the festivals and the Sabbath out of their original, natural context and linking them up, instead, with history? The answer leads us into the very heart of Judaism.

In the pagan view of life, still very much alive even in sophisticated twentieth century, man is chained to the blind necessities, and inexorable rhythms, of nature. Nature is a wheel that eternally turns on its own axis, apparently going nowhere but merely repeating itself. Man is bound to that wheel. As all things sprout up, bloom and then fade into the nothingness of the bosom of nature, out of which they emerge, so is man and all his works fated to perpetual repetition.

A profound pessimism, as might be expected, permeated the pagan view of life. If all was eternal repetition, what ultimate hope could there be? The final force of reality was the blind inexhaustible generative power of nature, the power of generation and regeneration. Each of the forces of nature was ruled by a god: the rain, the sun, the earth, etc. The

85

gods themselves annually traversed nature's eternal cycle of birth, growth, death and rebirth. It was these occasions that ancient pagan man celebrated. The function of his religion was to appropriate to himself, through ritualistic magic, something of the power of the gods. If he distinguished himself in this life by the appropriation and manifestation of such power, then after death he would be elevated to the status of a god.

The ethical, historical monotheism of Judaism marked a total rejection of paganism. The goal of man was not the appropriation of power but rather the fulfilment through righteousness, justice and peace of the divine purpose. Israel was chosen to be the people that would mark the way towards that goal. In its life, as manifested through its history and character, it would serve as a prototype of future humanity.

Its history was dramatically expressed through its festivals. Passover signified the redemptive power of God and the ideal of freedom. It celebrated the experience and the faith that God's power is manifest in the striving for freedom. Incidentally, it was, according to the prophet, not Israel alone whom God had redeemed: "Did I not bring up Israel from Egypt, and the Philistines from Kaphtor and Aram from Kir?" (Amos 9-7).

Shavuot commemorates the giving of the Torah and Israel's entrance into the covenant with God to strive to be a kingdom of priests and a holy nation. A genuine society must be based on an acceptance of the moral law (the Ten Commandments).

Sukkot is the recollection of the trials and tribulations of the years of wandering in the wilderness. The great goal in this instance, the Promised Land, must be preceded by periods in which the faith of men is tested. Again and

86

again in the wilderness, Israel was all but ready to abandon the goal and return to the bondage of Israel. All peoples are subjected to such tests, even mankind as a whole.

Thus, though the three festivals are rooted in the specific history of Israel, in their broader context they speak in universal terms. They express not alone the past, but the future of man in the wrestling with his destiny. Each of them carries overtones of universal meaning: "You shall not oppress the stranger, for you know the soul of the stranger, for you were strangers in the land of Egypt."

"Why," the rabbis ask, "was the Torah given in the wilderness of Sinai, rather than in the land of Israel?" Their answer is: "Just as the wilderness is the possession of no particular people, but is accessible and available to all, so is the Torah available to all." During the festival of Sukkot seventy sacrifices were brought in the Temple. These sacrifices, according to rabbinic tradition, were brought on behalf of the seventy nations of the world.

While the Sabbath represents no historical event (the creation of the world is cosmic), it too receives historical meaning in the Jewish tradition. The peace and joy of the Sabbath, the cessation from vexatious labor—all these were meant to be a foretaste of the world to come, the time when the pains, sorrows and frustrations of history will have been overcome.

In all truth, I must add that while the emphasis in the Jewish calendar is on the historical dimension of experience, there is an element of nature, though subordinate, that ought be noted.

Passover was the time of the bringing of the offering of the early spring harvest. *Shavuot* is still designated as the Festival of First Fruits, and *Sukkot*, with its *Lulav* and *Etrog* marks the fall harvest. For man lives in the dimension of both nature and history. But it is essentially in the latter sphere that human destiny must be worked out.

Let us bring the latter assertion down to the level of the concrete and see it in the perspective of our own time. The day is not distant when, thanks to modern technology, the possibility of material abundance for all men will be reality. Will human problems have then been solved? Our own experience of an affluent society in the post World War II period should indicate that, if anything, our problems—whether international in scope, or personal—will grow in magnitude and complexity. History does not cease when man's natural needs are met. In a sense, it really begins at that point. The question will still be: How does man live in peace and freedom and individual fulfillment, with purpose and dignity? This, only history can answer.

In sum, then, the Sabbath and the Jewish festivals are totally indigenous to the soil of the Jewish tradition. But because they have emerged out of a profound vision of God and human destiny, they speak a language all men can understand.

**Beginning
A
New
Year
In
The
Fall**

THERE IS, at first glance, something strikingly incongruous about beginning a New Year when the world of nature begins to decline and fade. Are we not children of nature, and should not our life be attuned to her rhythms? Would not fresh beginnings best be made in the spring of the year, when new life stirs and courses through the physical world? Indeed, so it was in all ancient pagan religions. The New Year did begin in the spring, synchronized to the revival of the natural world. The Jewish choice of the fall as the most propitious time for drawing a line and beginning again, is clearly not a haphazard one. The "natural" New Year is the spring. Rosh Hashanah in the fall, is meant to convey a lesson. What is that lesson?

The doctrine of the Stoics (the ancient Greek school of philosophy) that man should live in harmony with nature is really the abstract formulation of an old, universal, pagan concept. All nature—indeed, all existence—the pagan believed, was governed by a blind, inexorable fate to which even the gods were subject. This idea found its most dramatic expression in the world of classical Greek drama (Oedi-

89

pus, for example), though it informed every aspect of life. The image of man in paganism is primarily that of a victim. Man is bound by iron-clad necessity. He might occasionally defy the gods as did Prometheus, but such defiance invokes sure, and pitiless, Nemesis.

Paganism still flourishes in all kinds of deterministic philosophies. Man, we are told, is nothing more than the product of his heredity or environment. He is controlled by his glands or his libido (Freudianism), or by the methods of economic production (Marxism). In any case, he is still the victim of a world he never made.

Judaism was the first life-view to challenge paganism. Man, it proclaimed, is not chained to necessity. He is not simply the child of nature, bound by its blind powers and dominations. Man can transcend nature for he is a creature of a Creator who Himself stands beyond nature. There is an area of choice available to man. It is the animal, the true child of nature, that is caged by the narrow scope of blind instincts. Indeed, there is something in man that leads him, again and again, to transcend his natural appetites, and to hold them in check. There is something within us that bids us again and again to strive to incorporate into our lives the true, the good and the beautiful. This inner striving is a gift that reveals something of the nature of the giver—God.

So then, New Year in September or October is a version of Judaism's eternal protest against paganism. Nature may be going into its long sleep. But for man, free in spirit and unbound by Nature's necessities, these days mark a new, fresh beginning, a summoning of our moral and spiritual energies, a resolution and aspiration towards nobler aims, a gathering of faith and courage for the days ahead; in other words—Rosh Hashanah.

90

Again, consider the curious date of this new Jewish year, 5720. Christianity reckons time from the birth of Jesus, 1959. The coming of each year directs the mind of the Christian towards what Christianity regards as the central event in history, the time when history really began. According to Jewish tradition, 5720 represents the creation of the world. Rosh Hashanah is the birthday of the world. Hence, it would orient the mind of the Jew toward the world and its Creator. Can any view be wider, more universal than that?

What Is Sin?

SIN IS a word that has virtually dropped out of the vocabulary of modern man. We speak of mistakes, of errors, of failures, our own and those of others, but rarely, if ever, do we say, "I have sinned," or "it is a sin." Indeed, so vague has the word become that we would hardly know how to define it. And yet, Yom Kippur stands or falls on the proposition that sin is agonizingly real, that repentance is an ever-present possibility, and that atonement is attainable. The truth of that proposition will occupy us in this letter.

Sin, I would define as the alienation of man, willful or unintentional, from the three-fold source of reality: himself, his fellowman and God. One inevitably leads to the other as surely as the day follows the night, for all three—the self, the other, and God, are all coordinates of the axis of reality.

What is alienation? How does a man become estranged from his own true being? Some introspection and observation will supply the answer. Our basic primary need, though we often fail to recognize it, is the need to be affirmed, accepted or loved. How could it be otherwise?

Before we are born, in the embryo, we know perfect integration with our environment. We are an integral, organic part of it. Then comes birth and we are thrust out into the world with the destiny of achieving independent existence, and the manifest destiny of achieving a higher form of integration with our human and physical environment. Such, however, are the complexities of life, and such the difficulties of attaining that new and higher harmony, that more often than not we are frustrated. The environment does not respond to our needs—physical and psychological—promptly or fully. The infant, not fed on time, screams in anger. The infant, left alone by its mother, cries, out of fear and loneliness. The adult response to frustration is to grab, to fight, to struggle for power and domination, and, if need be, to cheat, to lie, etc. All of these responses are the perverse means of achieving the basic human need of acceptance, affirmation and love.

Let me make that plain. A person strives for status and prestige. Why? Because status and prestige make one feel accepted and respected by others. Psychologically they give one, in a perverse sort of way, what love naturally yields, the feeling that we are needed and important—the affirmation of the ego, a perfectly normal, legitimate and inevitable human need. But, because we so often resort to an almost endless variety of perverse means: pride of possessions or beauty of intellect, flattery, hypocrisy, sensuality, greed, chicanery—to obtain what we need, we grow estranged from our essential self. The being that wants and needs nothing more than acceptance becomes a flatterer, a hypocrite, a sensualist, etc. We lose genuine contact with our real self, and we refuse to know it. For the acceptance and self-esteem we gain by these methods never satisfies us. Like neurotic hunger, eating merely increases our appetite. Thus, we play an assumed role for we lose confidence in our self and grow fearful that the person we really are will not gain the esteem and affection of others. Having lost touch with our real self—which we can no longer accept—we cannot establish genuine communication with others.

Hence, the estrangement from others. Refusing to accept ourselves, aye, refusing to know our true self, how can we accept and really get to know other people? Our relationships with other people grow fragile, mechanical, external, surface, never deep, profound and satisfying. For between us and them, there stands the whole complex apparatus of what I have called the perverse means.

Mark this down as axiomatic: Only a person who fully, and completely, accepts and knows himself—and who really does?—can know, and accept, other people. How can we genuinely like any one else if we do not like ourselves? The rejection we feel for ourself, we project on other people. "Look out for the man who hates himself," says Nietzsche, "you may be his next victim." Is it any wonder that so many people are hostile, aggressive, suspicious, jealous, and really unable to accept the success of others?

Thus, we grow alienated from fellowmen, and a sense of loneliness and isolation invades our lives, while all the time, deep down, we carry an unappeased longing for friendship, love and communion with our fellowmen. I would say, in this connection, that the final test of a society is not its ability to fully meet the material needs of its members (ours by that standard would be the most brilliant and successful human society history has ever known) but, rather, its ability to create and sustain a sense of community and human solidarity among its members. Modern collectivism, whether it be within a communist, fascist, or capitalist framework such as our own, is the false answer to the failure of modern society to achieve the sense of community. (In a

94

collectivist society, the individual feels he is nobody, and therefore depends upon his affiliation and virtual worship of his group as the spurious source for a sense of vicarious significance.)

Alienation of self leads as invincibly to alienation from God as it does to estrangement from fellowmen. Failing to affirm himself, and hence others, man can hardly help but fail to affirm God. God, as I have sought to indicate in other letters, is the ultimate ground of reality, the source of genuine being. It is only from our real self that we can have any apprehension of God.

Our Tradition expresses that truth in a variety of striking ways. Let me cite one or two. There is the biblical statement: "Man looks at the outward appearance, but God looks to the heart." Or, there is the beautiful line of the Psalmist, "Who shall ascend unto the mountain of the Lord and who shall stand in His holy place? He who has clean hands and a pure heart." Finally, there is the talmudic statement, "God desires the heart." Let me put it simply. It takes reality to apprehend reality.

This is the three-fold alienation which spells sin. You would mistake my meaning if you were to understand me as saying that some men are sinners (the flatterers, the hypocrites, the sensualists, the deceivers, etc.), and some are righteous. Not at all. I am rather saying what the Bible said a long time ago: "There is no man on earth so righteous who doeth good and sinneth not." Sin is an inevitable accompaniment of our human condition. For whoever achieves a permanently perfect harmony with self, with others and with God? There are, as Pascal once said, only the sinners who think they are righteous and the righteous who think they are sinners. Only in B movies do you find

95

people neatly divided into the two categories of "the good guys," and "the bad guys." On this score, Judaism speaks with an astringent realism. That is the whole point of the story in the Torah, that even Moses must be denied entrance into the Promised Land because of his sin. So then, Yom Kippur, with its confession of sin, is everlastingly relevant to all of us.

One final word. Contemporary writers do not use the word sin. They permit the lives of the characters they create to serve as the judgment and fate they bring upon themselves. But the condition they describe, by and large, is that of alienation brought on, either by man himself, or his society or both, in their interplay with each other. While their analysis and illumination of the theme is often profound and impelling, and much is to be learned from them, they offer little if any hope for the alienated man. Here, Judaism teaches a truth that the modern mind has yet to apprehend— the truth of the ever-present possibility of repentance. But, of that, more in my forthcoming letter.

Repentance

And

Atonement

PERHAPS you remember the line from the Rubaiyat: "The moving finger having writ, moves on; not all your piety and wit can lure it back to cancel half a line of it." The quotation will serve as our point of departure for our interpretation of repentance, the second of the triad of themes that constitutes the meaning of Yom Kippur. We do not generally put it as elegantly as Omar Khayyam did, but our attitude in the presence of acknowledged failure comes to the same thing. "No use crying over spilt milk." "What's done can't be undone.' "Try harder next time."

Through all these and similar expressions, there runs the unspoken assumption that the past, for good or for woe, is forever immovably fixed, and there is simply nothing we can do about it. It follows then, that its consequences are equally inescapable, and must work themselves out in our lives. If we have committed some serious offense, there is nothing we can do, turn and dodge as we will, that will stay our payment of the consequences. To feel regret, sorrow, shame, to foreswear such deeds in the future, to repent (and I shall presently explicate the term), is totally irrelevant.

You recognize perhaps, in the view presented, something quite familiar from the ancient Greek tragedian. For his

97

coming, those who were involved are in no wise thereby saved from punishment. The final word, however, of biblical religion is that repentance breaks, so to speak, the iron his crime of patricide, a deed he was fated to commit, Oedipus must be pursued by Nemesis from disaster to disaster, handing down the fatality to his misbegotten children. A simple sense of justice demands that where there has been sin, there must be punishment. Indeed, something akin to this view is to be found in the earlier stages of biblical religion. Hence, there is no concept of repentance, and no staying of divine retribution. Though Moses pleads that God forgive the people for their sin of making and worshipping the Golden Calf, and such forgiveness is presumably forth- the Talmud says: "He who truly repents is reckoned as if he had been born anew."

Now, the ancient view that I described above has its modern counterpart. Substitute guilt for the concept of Nemesis, and we have the contemporary analogy for the old Greek view. Psychologists tell us, and we can believe them, that it is the sense of guilt that drives so many people to acts and attitudes that in disguised form aim at self-punishment or self-destruction. A sense of guilt impels a man to repeat the act, or an analogous act, of which he feels guilty in the hope that this time it will bring him direct punishment. It is unrequited guilt that makes repeaters of many people. But to name a deep-set emotional stance is not, of course, to exorcise it. Guilt is one of the most intractable conditions besetting the human soul that the psychiatrist has to deal with.

And here, the Jewish concept of repentance enters. You

98

will recall that in my previous letter I defined sin as essentially estrangement, alienation; a loss of contact with reality, with self, with fellowman and, with God. Strikingly enough, the Hebrew term for repentance is *t'shuvah*, literally, "returning." To do *t'shuvah* means to return to, and to reaccept the reality from which one has strayed. While we confess our misdeeds on Yom Kippur, and enumerate them in great detail, their confession is tantamount to a repudiation of the self that committed them. Our confession does not, of course, cancel out whatever wickedness we may have perpetrated. It does not wipe the slate clean. It wipes the soul clean. We recoil, not at the deeds, but at the self that could have performed such deeds. This is the point of the talmudic statement quoted above to the effect that he who does *t'shuvah* is considered as if he had been born anew; he is a new person.

With astounding insight, the Jewish concept of *t'shuvah* goes even deeper. The tradition asserts that transgressions between a man and his neighbor Yom Kippur does not atone, unless a man first reconciles himself with the neighbor whom he has offended. That is to say, repentance is of no avail unless a man first establishes a new, and true, relationship with his fellowman. That, of course, is only possible if one first cuts through the falsities and pretenses that obscure his real self.

Yom Kippur does, however, atone for the sins that stand between man and God. How are we to understand divine forgiveness, and atonement?

As we have seen, sin produces guilt, the sense of unpaid debt, of obligation unfulfilled, of responsibility we have failed to meet. It thus points to someone before whom we stand in judgment and in whose presence we feel guilty.

In a word, it points to God. For without a standard by which
we measure our acts, there would be no sense of guilt. Without someone before whom we felt responsible, we could not
be oppressed by the burden of our failure to meet responsibility. In a word, these feelings point to God. But these very
feelings make it impossible for us to stand upright in the
presence of God. They are the wall that stands between us
and all reality, and God is the ultimate reality.

It is repentance, as we have seen, that gives us a new
and fresh grip upon our real self and this makes it possible
for us to feel reaccepted by God. Forgiveness, human and
divine, means re-acceptance, re-alignment, a new harmonious
relation in place of the former estrangement. "My sin
(guilt) is too great to bear....Thou hast driven me this day
from the earth and I shall be hid from Thy face." Sin
drives man to hide. After eating of the forbidden fruit and
hearing the voice of God in the garden, Adam and Eve
hide among the trees of the garden. *T'shuvah* makes it
possible for man to re-enter the presence of God and to
address Him in truth and sincerity.

The central theme of Yom Kippur, then, comes to grips
with one of the deepest aspects of human life. Given the
complexities and ambiguities that invest every aspect of
life, man, the finite being, must inevitably fail to fulfill the
highest possibilities of good available to him. Without an
honest facing of his perversities, a fresh reintegration
of his being, and a new contact with reality, his life must
become virtually unbearable. Evidence of that is the focal
importance Christianity attaches to the idea of Jesus taking
the sins of mankind upon himself. But the idea of vicarious
atonement, aside from its mythic aspects, carries unresolva-
ble moral ambiguities. How can anyone, from a moral

100

perspective, suffer for our sins and thereby attain forgiveness for us? In this area, Judaism involves us neither in myths nor moral obscurities; for Judaism has Yom Kippur.

**The
Seder—
Reflections
On
Its
Meaning**

C. S. LEWIS, the English philosopher and essayist, has a delightful essay entitled, "The Same Old Thing." In it, he reflects on that quirk of human nature which revolts against repetitiveness. Any experience, no matter how originally delightful or instructive, if repeated and rehearsed again and again, loses its fine edge and grows so utterly dull, that all it is likely to call forth from us is the exclamation—"What! The same old thing!?" The essayist insists that the reaction is as unreasonable as it is unwarranted. Certain experiences are diurnal, some come with a given periodicity and, yet, for all their repetitive character they manage to evoke awe and delight in us. The sun rises and sets every day. Spring comes with unfailing regularity. And, here, we add, so does *Pesach*.

No one, we aver, who has ever been privileged to participate in a *Seder*, conducted with grace and dignity, could possibly approach the holiday with the feeling that it is "the same old thing."

Like all things that run down deep into the human condition, *Pesach* is always the same, and yet always different. Indeed, it is precisely that blend of the familiar and the

102

novel that lends the *Seder* and *Pesach* their unfailing appeal. To which of the senses does it not appeal? What depth of memory, hope and faith does it not stir?

Let us consider a few. Little need be said of the gustatory magic of the *Seder* that alone makes "This night different from all other nights"—everything, from *matza* to *kneidlach*, to that exotic mixture of nuts, apple and wine (*charoset*).

But, of course, the sense of taste is the least of the matter. There are the *Seder* melodies ranging from the traditional chant of the *Mah Nishtanah* to the rollicking *Chad Gadya*. And not least of all, the sight of the entire family gathered around the *Seder* table groaning under the assortment of *Pesach* wine cups, decanters, candles, the symbolic foods, etc.

I do not derogate the senses but, after all, they are only the gateway to deeper experiences and confrontations. Consider, for example, the enormous perspective of time the *Seder* opens up to us. Almost every age of the Jewish past has its own association with *Pesach*—from the bondage in Egypt to the Battle of the Warsaw Ghetto (its Anniversary falls on the first *Seder* night). The Jewish historic experience in all its pathos and its glory resounds on *Seder* night—but not alone the unforgettable experiences. Actually, we re-enact at the *Seder* the ancient Jewish way of conducting a festival meal. For example, the invitation to the hungry and the needy to come and join us is a revival, if only for the one evening, of a practice, that according to the Talmud, was in vogue in Jerusalem 2,000 years ago.

If, on *Seder* night, we live, so to speak, in the past, it is only that the past might, to some extent, live in us for the rest of the year. And who shall deny that there are

103

aspects of one's past, individual and collective, that can be sources of strength and inspiration?

Ritual is drama of the most serious kind. But no dramatist worth his salt has his characters discuss or pronounce his theme in abstract, conceptual terms. Always the theme is embodied in the characters and the situation. Reflection and analysis, however, can make it explicit.

The *Seder* motif is the ritualistic enactment of the eternal theme of bondage and redemption, as reflected in the drama of ancient Israel's liberation from Egypt. The power that puts a thirst for freedom in man, the power that propels man, despite all his stubborn reluctance, to move towards freedom is an aspect of God.

Bondage has a thousand forms and faces. Fear, greed, a burden of guilt, even freedom itself, misconceived as just doing whatever you want, etc., can confine and inhibit a man or a people.

The *Seder* concludes on a note of hope: "Next year in Jerusalem." Jerusalem, of course, is more than a city. It is a symbol of the Jewish messianic dream: a world without fear, without war—a world of peace and brotherhood.

26

The Particular And The Universal

NEXT to Rosh Hashanah and Yom Kippur no festival in the Jewish year exercises so potent a hold on our people as does *Pesach*. We may confidently assume that Jews who do not participate in some *Seder* on *Pesach* Eve constitute a negligible minority. Even the left-wing Kibbutzim in Israel where religious observance throughout the years is noticeably absent, conduct a *Seder* with great eclat. (It has been noted that the traditional elements in the latter *Sedarim* are on the increase in the past few years.) Speculation on the fact that the observance of *Pesach*, unlike other Jewish religious traditional practices, grows apace rather than declines, should prove revealing, and perhaps, even offer some clue to the inner meaning of Judaism. Or, in the traditional words of the *Haggadah*, one might well ask, "Why, indeed, is this night different from all other nights in the year?"

Family togetherness, the first and obvious distinguishing feature of the *Seder*, brings us to the threshold of the answer. The reality of Judaism and its appeal become most vivid and evocative when it is experienced and mediated through the group and, most emphatically, when it is the human group with which one has universal bonds, seen and unseen. Throughout the *Haggadah*, the emphasis is on the plural:

"Slaves were *we* unto Pharaoh in Egypt . . ." "And they oppressed *us* and the Lord saw *our* affliction and *our* distress." It is not alone that the *Haggadah* is written from the point of view of the group; even its most ancient form of observance, as prescribed in the Torah is directed towards the family or the clan.

What is the spiritual meaning of this singular fact—this emphasis on the social aspect of Judaism? As we see it, it is two-fold. Jewish religion, in its basic orientation, is not the revelation of an individual to individuals. Unlike Jesus and Mohammed, Moses first asks the people at Sinai whether they will accept God's law and undertake the task of becoming "a kingdom of priests and a holy nation." In the days of Ezra, to offer another biblical example, only when the assembled people agree to accept the Torah as their constitution does it become binding. In other words, Judaism is a teaching inseverably related to the historic, spiritual experience and self-commitment of the Jewish people. To this day, a Jew in prayer approaches God not as a discrete individual, but as a person aware that he stands within the context of a specific society whose antecedents are rooted in the remote past. Our classic prayer opens with the worlds, "Blessed art Thou, our God, and God of our fathers, God of Abraham, God of Isaac and God of Jacob."

Pagan man saw God most vividly in the phenomena of nature. Christianity sees Him in the person of a God-Man, Judaism experiences God through the experience, character and destiny of the people of Israel.

At the *Seder*, we sense not alone the universal value of family communion, but our family as a unit in the people of Israel, a family that in some measure is stamped by the experience, character and destiny of our people.

But there is another side to the coin, and that side bears the inscription of the eternal, universal quest for freedom. Whether we are aware of it or not, *Pesach's* perennial appeal is its power to evoke and give symbolic release to that impulse. We may never have articulated the idea, but we do something more convincing. We experience and manifest it in an endless variety of ways. There is something in us, and it is the better part of us, that strives to overcome all the trammels and limitations placed upon us by the exigencies of nature and society. Earthbound, man dreamed of flying and defying the force of gravity. Mortal man dreams and longs for immortality. Often dragooned by social pressures, we day-dream of defying them. Coerced by instinct and habit, we attempt to curb and master them. We witness today the amazing election various peoples make—choosing freedom and the mastery of their own destiny rather than bread and security. (A colonial people that gains its political independence and cuts its ties with the mother country is in for a rough time economically.)

So then, the hunger for freedom is indefeasible and its appeal is perennial. For us Jews, its powerful, external symbol is the dramatization of the Exodus story enacted at the *Seder*. Thus, *Pesach* unites two basic, yet disparate, elements of Judaism—its historic individuality, what may be called its consciousness of self, and its universal element, man's passion and prizing of freedom. Hence, to be a Jew means to be, at one and the same time, the most individual and particularistic of men and the most universal.

Why Is This Night Different?

27

W HY IS this night different from all other nights?" You probably remember the *Mah Nishtanah* as a child at the *Seder*. Now, as *Pesach* approaches, I would like to broaden the traditional question so that its scope embraces not only the ritual of the *Seder* but the whole sweep of Judaism. Is Judaism different, and if it is, whereof do its essential differentia consist? Finally, is the ideal of One World incompatible with a socially, religiously, and culturally differentiated society?

Obviously, the forms and practices of Judaism are distinctive. A religious celebration at home, such as the *Seder*, in which all members of the family participate, including the youngest child, is quite unknown among other religious communities. But do these particular forms of observance embody local, particularist values, or are these values universally meaningful?

The concept of God as expressed in the *Seder*, as He who redeems man from physical and spiritual bondage, is clearly universal in import, though it grew out of a particular episode in Jewish history. The Jewish prophets realized this ages ago. "Did I (God) not bring up Israel from Egypt, the Philistines from Caphtor and the Arameans from Kir?"

(Amos 9:7). Are we then to conclude that Judaism is particularistic in form and universal in content, that the basic concepts of the Jewish religion are identical with those of all ethical, monotheistic religions? Such a conclusion would be premature and wide of the mark.

Let me illustrate by analogy. The basic human traits— fear, love, anger, etc.—are universal, yet no two individuals are alike. In each of us, these traits arrange themselves in patterns so distinctive as to give us a unique personality. Some of us are outgoing; some are introverted. Though all of us contain in our make-up elements of both extraversion and introversion, it is the *tout ensemble* that counts; our personality pattern molded in large measure by our particular history and background.

So it is with all religious cultures, and with Judaism. Hence, all religions, for all their similarities, are different each from the other; different in mood, in temper and in emphasis. (Even within the same basic religious tradition there are broad differences. Thus, the atmosphere and mood of Catholicism are poles apart from that of liberal Protestantism.)

Beyond this general consideration, Judaism is unique in another regard. For all the universality of its basic concepts—one God, a universal moral law, the dignity of man— Judaism has always been a religious culture of the Jewish people alone. The history of Judaism and the history of the Jewish people are inextricably bound up together. Our peoplehood and our religious culture are co-terminous; they began at the same time and if ever they should cease they would end at the same time. The non-Jew who adopts Judaism becomes thereby not only a Judaist, a participant in Jewish religion, but also a member of the Jewish people.

109

To seek, as some Jews do, notably the American Council of Judaism, to sever one from the other is to pronounce doom on both. "He who excludes himself from the Jewish community," reads the Haggadah, "thereby denies the basic principle." The basic principle is that we are a people and our peoplehood is based on a common history which extends from the Exodus of Egypt to this day. The dynamic underlying principle of that history has been a self-commitment, to seek to fulfill the biblical injunction "And thou shalt be unto Me a kingdom of priests and a holy nation."

In a sense, the foregoing has already anticipated the answer to our third question. At the present stage of history, One World cannot possibly mean one language, one religion, one culture, etc. This ideal makes sense only if we understand it to mean a mutual tolerant respect for the differences that characterize the various peoples that make up the family of man.

Again let me illustrate by analogy. Only he who has been blessed by the experience of having loving parents of his own can have genuine respect and understanding for another's devotion to his parents. Only he who is rooted in his own community of faith and to whom its symbols are precious can genuinely respect another man's devotion to his own community. If we possess no such rootedness, then another's devotion must appear mysterious, something strange and unreasonable and, hence, suspect and inwardly resented.

**Spirit
In
An
Age
Of
Power**

28

OF ALL the battles and wars in which our people were engaged in ancient times, only two remained permanently fixed in Jewish historical consciousness and thus entered the calendar of annual remembrance. One was the disastrous defeat at the hands of the Romans, culminating in the end of The Second Jewish Commonwealth (70 C.E.), and marked, to this day, by the Feast of the Ninth Day of Av (*Tisha B'Av*). That mournful recollection, naturally, reinforced by the long years of exile, served to keep ever fresh and alive the hope and faith of eventual restoration. Thus, out of the ashes of defeat, there emerged the unquenchable embers of hope, spectacularly rekindled in our own day, through the re-establishment of the State of Israel. The other was the startling victory of the Maccabees over the Syrian Greeks that led to the recovery of Jewish independence and religious freedom. It, of course, is celebrated as Chanukah.

Now it is a curious and striking fact that the Jewish religious tradition in its observance and recollection of both wars, that against the Romans, and that against the Syrian Greeks, almost completely neglects the sheer military aspects of the struggle. Were it not for historical sources preserved

111

outside the scope of the traditional Jewish record, we would know virtually nothing of the facts and figures of what were life and death struggles of our people in ancient times. Jewish historical consciousness sought the meaning of both events, not on the level of the physical, power, numbers, weapons, tactics, etc., but on the spiritual level.

As if to underscore the point, a prophetic passage (*Haftorah*) was chosen for the Sabbath of Chanukah that concludes with the words, "Not by power, nor by might, but by My spirit, saith the Lord." In an age in which man has unleashed almost limitless physical power by splitting the atom and may remake—or possibly unmake—the world by the use of that power, the prophet's words exalting the spirit seem dated, indeed. But it is not alone in the physical realm that spirit—and the word embraces such allied concepts as ideas, convictions, principles and faith—has been radically downgraded. Jacques Barzun in his recent book, *The House Of Intellect,* cries havoc against the steadily diminishing role assigned to intellect even in the academic world and the creative arts.

Contemporary prepossessions aside, a long careful look at history should convince us that what has changed human destiny again and again, has been the eruption of new ideas. Karl Marx swallowing dust in the reading room of the British Museum Library a century ago, and writing *Das Kapital* and his *Communist Manifesto,* changed the history of the world—for the worse, we believe, but change it he did. Freud, ruminating on the meaning of dreams, discovered the unconscious and added a new dimension to almost every field of human knowledge. Need the examples be multiplied?

Not alone in the realm of ideas has the spirit shown itself mightier than marching phalanxes of armed men. An

112

idea held with passion—that is, a faith—has opened, time and again, new chapters in human history. When Herzl declared at the First Zionist Congress in 1897, "To-day, I have founded the Jewish State," the most intelligent minds of his day put him down—if they took any notice of him at all—as a harmless crackpot. The whole history of Zionism is demonstration of the invincible power of the idea, clothed in nothing but truth and armed with faith.

I know not how else to begin to understand the survival of our own people except that it was possessed by the monotheistic idea wedded to the belief in its full realization only in messianic times.

So, for me, Chanukah is the occasion for the re-affirmation and celebration of a basic Jewish attitude: the faith that the ultimate factor in human life, the absolute factor, if you will, is the power of the spirit—the intangibles of convictions that grip men's souls and stir men's minds and hearts.

Here, I think I hear a question in your mind. "In affirming the power of the spirit in human affairs, you fail to reckon with the decisive fact that an individual or a group might well be possessed by a spirit of conquest, exploitation and destructiveness. Hitler, too, was moved by a powerful conviction, one that brought unbounded ruin and suffering to millions of people." The question is fair enough. Let us, however, analyze it.

Hitler's or Stalin's convictions, as the event proved, were aimed not at the strengthening and diffusion of spirit, but rather at its destruction and ultimate extermination. Their convictions and principles were merely a tool aimed at the acquisition of naked power. Once attained, the realm of the spirit—culture and religion—could be, and indeed were, curbed and suppressed insofar as they posed a threat to the maintenance and extension of the power they sought. A true commitment to the spirit, the realm of ideas and ideals, means that I desire that realm to grow and attain increasing hold on men's minds and souls. The only proper method available for the spiritual in its effort to maintain itself is that of persuasion and reason, not force or threat of force. Very simply stated, spiritual ends can only be attained by spiritual means.

All of which brings us back to the verse from the *Haftorah* of Shabbat Chanukah. The messianic goals the prophet foresees will be brought about "not by might, nor by power, but by My Spirit, saith the Lord of Hosts." Now, I trust, it is clear why in our observance of Chanukah, the ancient military victory of the Maccabees was transformed in the Tradition to an occasion for the exaltation of that which truly makes man human—the spiritual.

Chanukah

And

Miracles

THE SECOND *bracha* (blessing) for the lighting of the Chanukah candles concludes with the words, "Who performed miracles for our fathers in those days at this season."

My dictionary defines a miracle as a supernatural event, one that presumably defies the laws of nature. If science has taught us anything, it is that there are no breaks in nature. Water never runs uphill, the sun never rises in the west, iron does not float—because these phenomena would require a suspension of the laws of gravity, specific density, etc. From all empiric observation and experience, the physical laws by which the world operates are never broken, never suspended, never defied.

Are miracles, then, in the realm of the fairytale, suitable perhaps for children, but not for mature minds? Specifically, what of the miracle of Chanukah? (The story of the sacred cruse of oil which burned for eight days, though the oil it contained sufficed only for one day.)

Here is my answer. Judaism does not stand or fall by a belief in the reality of supernatural events in the past as recorded in the Bible. I can be a very devout Jew and yet refuse to believe, for example, that a stick can be turned

115

into a snake. What does the Torah want to express when it describes how God formed the staff of a Moses into a serpent? Clearly, it meant to express the omnipotence of God. This I most firmly believe. How could God be God without being omnipotent? To me, God's omnipotence is expressed not through violation of the laws of nature that inhere in the world He created, but in the uniform, regular, unbreakable character of these very laws.

To me, miracles are not dim events supposed to have taken place in the distant past. Our prayer book speaks of "Thy miracles that are ever with us." There are miracles all around us. (Not in the sense of supernatural events, but in the sense of testimony to a beneficent, creative, intelligent Power.) The emergence of human life on this planet is a miracle, though we have theories as to how it happened. The sustaining of human life is no less a miracle. (How many species have become extinct in the course of the evolutionary process?) The very fact that there is an order, a system—be it biological or psychological—that is a miracle, a testimony to the Supreme Intelligence.

At this season of the year, however, I become acutely aware of another "miracle"—the power of the human spirit, infused with a sense of righteous purpose to overcome sheer physical might. To me, as a Jew, the story of Chanukah is the supreme illustration of this universal truth, though, of course, there are others, both individual and collective: these are the stars that shine in the darkness that cover so much of human history. The wonder is that the stars can penetrate the darkness.

Why should such spirit ultimately overcome massive power? I have only one answer. This is the miracle that God wrought for our fathers in those days at this season.

116

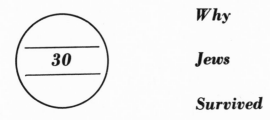

Why

30

Jews

Survived

OUR THEME this month is a hardy perennial, as fascinating to students of history as it is pertinent to every Jew concerned for the perpetuation of the Jewish people. Why, of all the welter of peoples of the ancient world, did the Jews alone survive? If we had the answer to that question, and the answer fell within the scope of human effort, would we not hold the key to the Jewish future in our hands?

But there, precisely, is the rub. Usually, the answer is clouded in terms of transcendent mystery, and Jewish survival is made to appear an insoluble enigma, a defiance of the laws of history. Emotionally moving as such a statement might be, it is obviously of no pragmatic value. For all its mystic glow, it sheds no usable light or insight on the problem of Jewish survival today. Moreover, it is a needless obscuring of what is crystal clear.

The Jewish people survived because Judaism fulfilled an important function in the life of the individual Jew. It served a purpose; it answered a purpose; it answered a need, or rather, a complex of needs. If Judaism should fail to fulfill a function it will decay and vanish. Jews cannot survive the death of Judaism. (Only in *Alice in Wonderland* does the smile of the Cheshire cat survive the cat.)

To live means to function. This is a reversible proposition. As long as something functions (fulfills a need) it is assured of life. Obviously, Judaism would not have survived all these years—and with it the Jewish people—unless it did meet some basic and indispensable needs of Jews. So then, if we are concerned that the Jewish people endure, the basic question is what function can Judaism serve in our lives today? (Not, how can we save Judaism, but how can it save us. A Judaism that has to be saved isn't worth saving!)

I suggest that Judaism today, as always, has three prime functions in our lives. It can and does affirmatively and meaningfully relate us to the three principal dimensions of human life: the cosmic, the social, and the individual.

As for the first of these dimensions, it should be recalled that the word "religion" comes from the Latin *religio*, meaning, to bind, to relate. By its God concept, Judaism teaches us, and inculcates in us (through its services, festivals, sacred literature and rites), the faith that human existence has supernal significance. We are not, Judaism teaches, an accidental collocation of atoms. There is in us a spark of the divine (man created in the image of God). On any other basis, man is a fugitive stranger in a world that cares least for what man himself cares for most. Anyone who says he does not need that assurance is whistling in the cosmic dark, or talking off the intellectual cuff, and not from his own inner depth.

Again, Judaism profoundly responds to our need of being part of a meaningful, significant society with which we can identify emotionally. (Modern nationalism is a comparatively new phenomenon. Limitations of space preclude me from discussing the question why nationalism does not, except in perverted dangerous forms, meet this need.) The

118

society of which our Judaism makes us a part is, of course, the Jewish people. I cannot pause to dwell upon the "meaningful" aspects of Jewish history, past and present, that serve to give sweep and significance to our lives in the social aspect. Briefly stated, it is both a humbling and an exalting experience to realize that one is a member of a people whose ancient history is the sacred history of a large portion of mankind.

Finally, in its moral imperatives, Judaism meets our individual need for a dynamic that will help us in our efforts to transcend ourselves. There is something within us that will not permit us to permanently live on the natural level of self-indulgence and self-gratification. We seek, now and again, to achieve the moral level of "Thou shalt love thy neighbor as thyself," though we fail more often than we succeed. The ethical teachings of Judaism and above all the example of its community of righteous, can sustain and inspire us in our faltering quest to achieve our highest moral potential.

It may take some introspection to discover these needs within ourselves. Indeed, they are so deeply rooted within us that we may consciously hardly be aware of their existence. The fact, however, that Jews who live a Jewish life experience a sense of joy, indicates that some basic function in their lives is being performed by Judaism. In a word, Judaism has the power to speak to *us*, here and now.

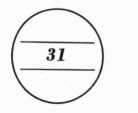

The House We Live In

THE OTHER day I had an experience that touched off a kind of mental chain reaction. A young man, in his early twenties, came into my study and told me that he had been reared as a Catholic, but that for the past two years he had found Catholicism unacceptable and that he wanted to consider becoming a Jew. To my question, whether he was about to marry a Jewish girl and, hence, sought conversion, the answer was a resounding "no!" It was at this point, as I began to reflect, that the chain reaction set in.

Under ordinary circumstances, is it conceivable, I asked myself, that a Jewish young man, finding Judaism unacceptable for one or another reasons (real or imaginary) would want to cease being a Jew? Conceivably, a Jew might give up practising the Jewish religion after finding himself in sharp disagreement with one or more of the basic principles of Judaism, and yet, it would take something even more than that to make him seek to change his identity. He would have to renounce himself, the parents from whom he is sprung, and beyond them, the whole line of Jewish ancestry back to Abraham and, finally, his contemporary fellow Jews. Clearly, being Jewish is more than a set of religious

120

beliefs and practices, just as a human being is more than his intelligence or psychological make-up, even though these are indispensable elements in one's humanity.

Hence, the equation, Catholic, Protestant and Jew, for all its homely, everyday practicability, does not begin to exhaust the reality implied in the word, Jew. And if further evidence were needed, there is the practice that a non-Jew who converts to Judaism is traditionally given a Hebrew name ben *Avraham* (son of Abraham), a token of the fact that he is henceforth to be considered a descendant of Abraham, and that he, like all Jews, can now say, *Abraham Avinu*—"Abraham our father."

So then, this is the basic, ineluctable fact: One is born a Jew, and is spiritual heir to Judaism, as much as one is physical heir to one's parents. One can be a good son or a bad son, but he cannot cease being a son. (Theoretically, Jewish law regards even a Jew who has apostacized and converted to another religion as a Jew; a bad one, of course, but withal a Jew.) What one does with one's heritage: rejects it, accepts it in toto, selects from it, cultivates it, scorns or neglects it, depends on oneself.

Honesty commands that whatever stance one takes toward Judaism—the heritage to which we are the only legitimate and direct heirs by reason of our faith—one must first understand it. One cannot reasonably reject what one does not truly understand. And the plain truth of the matter is that few people really understand Judaism. Elementary Jewish education at its best— to what may it be compared? To a child reading Lamb's *Tales of Shakespeare* (incidentally, a classic in its own right), and on that basis passing judgment on the inexhaustible richness of Shakespeare. (Unfortunately, we do not yet have the elementary text books

121

in Judaism that begin to approach the fascination of the book by Charles Lamb.)

So, then, it seems to me that an attitude of humility, an openness of mind—more, a willingness and eagerness to understand, befits most of us on the subject of Judaism or, for that matter, on any subject.

Permit me to offer an illustration by way of elucidating a small aspect of Judaism in the Bible. Recalling some biblical stories—say the story of Adam and Eve in the Garden of Eden—and then learning something about evolution, cultural anthropology, etc., how deceptively simple it must be to dismiss the biblical account as just so much ancient, fanciful legend, as much unrelated to reality, as say, Alice in Wonderland. And one's account with the Bible is forthwith closed. But, then, perhaps one recalls that Freud found some of his most profound insights already expressed in ancient Greek myths.

Now, of course, the Garden of Eden story is myth, but may it not contain permanent truth, distilled out of the deepest recesses of human consciousness and experience, even though it is expressed in mythical form, and not in conceptual terms? (A picture, poem or piece of music, it must be remembered, do not flow out of conceptual terms though they can, once having been produced, be interpreted and understood in those terms.)

Now, the Garden of Eden story offers, among other things, an insight—and a valid one—into the source of human evil. "And you shall be like God, knowers of good and evil," says the Serpent, meaning that man will be omnipotent. Man's desire to be like God, an absolute in himself, self-contained, with all possibilities always open, the refusal to regard oneself as limited, as commanded either by God or

122

others—that is the source of the evil we do. (Reflect for a moment on the megalomaniacs of history and the crimson tide they let loose upon the world, knowing no law but their own will.)

These few sentences hardly begin to plumb the depths of the truth the biblical myth contains. Hopefully, it is enough to recognize that its dismissal as ancient fairy tale, with nothing to teach us, is the sheerest kind of sophomoric superciliousness. Hopefully, too, it is enough to indicate that whatever our particular problem with one or another aspect of the Jewish tradition, an open mind, eager for more light, is called for, not a rush to conclusions.

Lest I be misunderstood: I am not advocating the total Jewish tradition; only an Orthodox Jew could do that conscientiously. But I am advocating the tradition as a whole. It is the house we have inherited. It may need some renovation here and there, some modernization. But one thing we cannot do; we cannot dispossess ourselves.

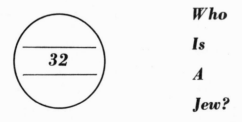

Who Is A Jew?

THE simplest words are the hardest to define. Anti-disestablishmentarianism—the longest word in the English language, is easy. But try and define precisely such one syllable words as *to* or *of* or *is*. The semanticists identify the score or more of meanings in each of these everyday mono-syllables. No wonder, then, that the question recently raised, "Who is a Jew?" has brought forth a plethora of discussion and debate, and no consensus is yet in sight. And there can be none until we carefully sort out the various categories to which the term Jew belongs.

Let me illustrate the latter point. Suppose we were to ask, "What is a man?" Clearly, the term man can be described on a number of levels; each is the necessary condition for the level beyond it. Approximately, let us call the levels the physical, emotional, intellectual, social. A being can be called man only if he possesses the physical structure of humankind. Nothing can substitute for these. If, somehow, a chimpanzee could be forced to acquire the basic emotional-intellectual equipment of a child, would that make it a man? Obviously not. Similarly, then, a being that possessed human physical structure yet did not possess human emotional-intellectual capacities—say a Mongolian idiot—would still be a man, even if a tragically poor specimen. Finally, a man can be described as a being who identifies himself as akin and related to other human beings—the social capacities.

Of course, these are not the only possible criteria. Thinkers from Aristotle down have defined man in dozens of different ways. Some speak of him as *Homo faber* (man the tool-maker); others, as *Homo sapiens* (man the thinker); the Bible, as the creature made in the image of God. The essential point is that there is a hierarchy of levels, each presuming and dependent upon the one below it.

Now, let us apply this analogy to the question at hand: Who is a Jew? Just as anyone is a man who is born of human parents, so is anyone a Jew who is born of Jewish parents. (Hence you do not become a Jew by being Bar Mitzvah or confirmed. Both ceremonies are simply meant to signify one's joining the adult community of Israel.) But because being a Jew is more than a purely physical fact— in other words, spiritual fact—one can become a Jew by conversion to Judaism. (I readily grant that my analogy with the term "man" does not cover this particular matter. But then, no analogy can be perfect.) Interestingly enough, the convert to Judaism is given a Hebrew name "son (or daughter) of Abraham," the latter, of course, being the Father of the Jewish people. It is to say that the convert by accepting Judaism becomes an adopted son or daughter of the Jewish people. In other words, one cannot accept the faith without the people, nor the people without the faith. Conceivably, a born Jew or adopted Jew might renounce the Jewish faith by affiliating himself with some other religious community. According to Jewish law, such a person is still a Jew, just as a person who renounces his parents

125

still remains a son or daughter, albeit a bad one.

On the next level, a Jew is one who shares the emotional, intellectual, moral and spiritual values of Judaism. Obviously, here there can be no precise measurement, and wisely enough Jewish tradition sets no precise universal measurements. To one person, certain values and practices of Judaism (*mitzvah*) will make a particular appeal; to another person, the emphasis will be some other aspect of Judaism. The decisive matter is that a person regard Judaism as the source whence his deepest values come and to which, accordingly, he owes loyalty.

Finally, our social capacity is our recognition of other Jews as akin and related to us. In other words, we identity ourselves with the Jewish people and we are concerned with its welfare and feel a sense of responsibility towards it. (Such special sense of identification with the Jewish people no more precludes our concern for the welfare of humanity generally, than does our special identification with the members of our respective families.)

Here, then, is my answer to the question, "Who is a Jew?" On the primary level, the question is answered. Perhaps like the analogous question "Who is a man?"—the more important one is, "What kind of a Jew?" Just as we strive to be the best kind of human being we can, so ought we strive to be the best kind of Jew. Indeed, implicit in our faith is the postulate that Judaism is our way of seeking the former goal. Those who have traveled that road before us came up with some extraordinary results: such human beings as the Prophets, Hillel, Maimonides, the Baal Shem Tov, etc. Just as Providence has given us a specific set of parents, so has it put us on this particular road. It is our task to walk it as nobly as we can.

126

**The
Jewish
Contribution
To
America**

I AM sure that you have often heard the statement that there is no fundamental opposition between the basic American ideals of equality, dignity of the individual, and freedom, and those proclaimed by Judaism long ago. The historian Lecky's statement: "Hebraic ideals were the mortar that cemented American democracy," sums up the matter. The statement is incontestable.

But like most truths, it is a practical truth and does not encompass, nor express, the total situation. It is my thesis that there are significant areas in which the actual values of American life do stand in radical irreconcilable opposition to those of Judaism. Further, the greatest single collective contribution we Jews can make to America lies not in the area in which Americanism and Judaism coincide, but in the sphere where they diverge. By seeking to advance these Jewish values—I shall presently specify them—we can make a unique, immeasurable contribution to the totality of American life. Great as have been our contributions to America as individuals—think, for a moment of the present situation in which two members of President-elect Kennedy's Cabinet, besides his personal adviser on scientific affairs, are Jews—

greater still can be that collective leaven that we can add to American life if we but have the wisdom and the courage to exemplify certain unique traits of the Jewish tradition.

Nor should we for a moment regard it as smacking of "Un-Americanism," to find ourselves, by reason of our tradition, dissenting from certain aspects of American life. No group of men ever loved their own people more passionately than did the ancient Jewish prophets, yet none were more severe and unrelenting in their criticism of their contemporaries. Yesterday's radical critics of American life—Whitman, Thoreau, Veblen, for example—are today's culture heroes. It is the narrowest, blindest, most provincial kind of thinking to imagine that American civilization stands at the acme of human perfection, and that we have nothing to learn from others. As the words themselves indicate, didn't we borrow pyjamas from the Japanese, coffee from the Turks and, to include the latest addition, pizza from the Italians? And so, too, in the realm of ideas and values, what is wrong with accepting larger truths, and more fruitful values, wherever we can find them?

Now, let me turn to a few specifics by way of illustration. The typical American is a pragmatist—practical minded, impatient, and essentially unconcerned with anything that does not directly help turn the wheels of industry, business, profession, entertainment, etc. His first question about anything is: "Of what use is it?" More and more today, our education reflects that bent. Education is increasingly regarded as a tool. The non-practical studies are being crowded out of the curriculum. Outside the halls of academe, the trend is even more pronounced. (Glancing through the card catalogue of a public library the other day, I found a half tray of index cards of books all beginning with the title

"How To"—everything from "How to Repair Your Car," to "How To Make Money in the Stock Market.")

Say what you will about Judaism, its literature, and institutions, there is in all of it a large, ineradicable element of impracticability. Not the least of the glories of Judaism is its concept of the Sabbath, one day out of seven in which nothing is made, nothing produced, or created. Was anything ever more impractical than that? Indeed, the ancient Romans—an eminently practical minded people—were so astounded by the Jewish observance of the Sabbath, that they concluded that the Jews must be innately a lazy people.

Or, take this historic, yet contemporary example of Jewish impracticability. Granted the urgent problem of Jewish homelessness and persecution in Europe in the first half of the 20th century. Why did the Jews have to pick on Palestine as the site of a Jewish national home, a barren desolate land, impoverished and infested with such Oriental diseases as malaria and trachoma, to say nothing of Arab suspicion and hostility? At one time, other areas of the world could have been had, virtually for the asking. The answer is: historic sentiment, ancient memories and millennial dreams and hopes—all highly impractical things.

These are values in life that cannot be reduced or incorporated into technology or earning a livelihood. These are moral, esthetic and spiritual—and it is of these that Judaism essentially consists. Without them in our life, we become an economic man, nothing more than an adjunct and a slave of the machine he has created. These values constitute man in depth, and help make us truly human.

To be sure, Judaism does not claim a monopoly on them, but we do have a long, and honorable, tradition in which they were cultivated with a passion that few people have

129

displayed. To abandon them, or leave off seeking to understand them and appropriate them into our lives, is not alone
to forsake that tradition; it would be a signal failure to
enrich America out of the resources of that tradition—an
America, to which we Jews both individually and collec-
tively, owe so much.

**The
Conspiracy
Of
Silence
On
Jewish
History**

34

FORGIVE my launching our theme on a personal note. If I begin with an experience of my own college days, it is only because you too, in your own way, may have shared it. In my courses in history—I think I took just about every one offered—I was always somewhat piqued to find that textbook references to Jewish history were as rare as they were meagre. They consisted of a few paragraphs in Ancient History, a paragraph perhaps on the Jews as intellectual middlemen in Medieval History, and virtually none in Modern History. I have long since gotten over my pique. Instead, I've tried to understand this weird phenomenon: a people with one of the longest continuous histories in the world, exceeded, perhaps, only by the Chinese, rates nothing more from the historians than a few passing references! It almost seems as if there were a conspiracy of silence on the part of the historians. What explains it?

There are, I think, a number of traditional assumptions—all of them demonstrably false—that account for the failure to reckon with Jewish history as part of world history. One of these assumptions harks back to the Christian viewpoint that the living heritage of Judaism, all that was vital and precious in it, was carried forward by Christianity, its legitimate heir and successor. Hence, with the coming of Christianity, Judaism *per se* ceased to be a factor in human history. Closely allied to this outlook, is the supposition that with the destruction of the Jewish State by the Romans in the year 70 C.E., the Jews ceased to be a people and became a religious sect. Conventional history deals with the history of nations and empires. Sectarian history is of interest only insofar as it impinges on national history.

Both assumptions are equally ungrounded. It can be demonstrated that quite apart from what Christianity took over from Judaism, the latter continued to exert a profound influence on the march of Western civilization. The two upheavals in Christendom—the Protestant Reformation and English Puritanism—both of which brought far-reaching political and social changes, had deep roots in Judaism as represented in the Jewish Bible. The periodic resurgence of the Jewish element in Christianity, invariably stimulated by the actual presence of Jews, has always signalled broad reverberations in the general political and social structure.

Even more directly, and most particularly, since the emancipation of Jews following the French Revolution, there has been a distinct Jewish influence on Western culture. That influence, exemplified by such names as Marx, Freud and Einstein, and by a myriad of lesser lights, has its roots in some of the basic axioms of the Jewish religion. That these men neither avowed nor formally practised Judaism does not alter the fact that their world outlook bears an obvious Jewish impress. Quite sketchily, it may be described as the faith in the equality of all men, the affirmation and attainment of justice in human affairs, an emphasis upon

132

this life, the here and now, and finally, the faith that the problems of life, insofar as they are solvable, are susceptible to reason.

All four propositions are, if you will, articles of faith. In themselves, they are not subject to rational proof. But they happen to be the way the Jew looks at the world. They are unique to Judaism in the sense that in no other religious culture do they occupy the central position they do in Judaism. Formally, Freud was an Austrian, Marx was a German (and baptized Jew, to boot), Einstein was a German, and later, an American. But can there be any doubt that the revolutions they wrought in mankind's outlook are to be traced, in good measure, to their Jewishness and to their political or even cultural citizenship?

I am not, of course, arguing that all history revolved around the Jewish people. That would be the sheerest kind of hallucinatory egoism. But I do insist that our actual role in history has been something quite different from what you will find in the history textbooks. All of the foregoing, however, is but a prelude to an even more pertinent question than any that can be raised about the Jewish role in civilization in the past. Is there a Jewish role in society today? Do we have a specific contribution to make? What is it?

My next letter will discuss these questions.

**The
Role
Of
The
Jew
Today**

35

MY LAST letter ended with a question: "Do Jews have a specific role to play in present day society?" This letter is devoted to sketching out the main lines of the answer to that question.

As I see it, our role is a threefold one and is operative in three spheres: religious, moral and social.

Judaism's monotheism is absolute and uncompromising. In both Protestant and Catholic Christianity the approach to God is through Jesus, however the figure of Jesus may be construed.

To borrow an old witticism, no Jew would ever think of worshipping another Jew. In Judaism it is inconceivable to think of God as ever assuming human form; for between God and man, there is an unbridgeable gulf in essence. The Bible and the Talmud speak of man drawing close to God through good deeds and prayer but never becoming God or Godlike.

The presence of Judaism in the world is a perpetual challenge and correction to any religion which is not a strict monotheism. There are important psychological corollaries to a strictly monotheistic religion. The latter tends

134

towards a humanistic theism, an attitude which emphasizes human possibilities. Let me illustrate by a message from Maimonides: "It is possible for any man to attain the level of illumination reached by Moses." Such statement is unthinkable in the Christian view, if the figure of Jesus is substituted for that of Moses. (Incidentally, the view of Judaism as a corrective to Christianity is one advanced by Paul Tillich, noted Christian theologian. Tillich, however, fails to trace out all the implications of his own position.)

What is the Jewish role in the moral sphere? Justice is the keystone of Jewish ethics. By contrast, the key criterion of the ancient Greek mind was esthetic. Indeed, to the cultured Greek the beautiful and the good were virtually equivalent. The poet John Keats summed up this view in his famous line: "Beauty is truth, and truth beauty, that is all ye know and all ye need to know." The Jew, on the other hand, had an unquenchable passion for justice. Abraham's agonized outcry (Genesis 18:25): "Shall not the Judge of all the earth do justly?" is a note that re-echoes throughout the Bible. History made us the classic victims of injustice, and thus bred into the marrow of our bones an unappeasable restlessness in the face of injustice. It is no accident that some of the outstanding leaders in movements of social protest and reform in the late 19th, and early 20th, centuries were Jews. It is no accident that Jews developed, and to this day maintain, a vast system of privately sponsored social services aimed to palliate the injustices and inequalities perpetrated by man and nature. It is no accident that Jews naturally tend to sympathize with the underdog, and generally maintain a liberal position on social questions.

In the social sphere, we are, by reason of our Jewishness, non-conformists. (People who don't like us call it clannish-ness.) Call it what you will, in a civilization that tends, alas, to ever greater uniformity we remain distinctive, different, perpetuating a tradition other than that of the dominant majority. Values in life are created by the process of differentiation, and not by the process of uniformity. Toynbee, in his monumental *Study of History*, has indicated as much in his description of creative minorities. The presence of the Jew is an added dike of protection against the swift running currents that tend to swamp all minorities and render society totalitarian in ethos and practice.

The foregoing is, of course, only the briefest outline. It is, however, enough to indicate that those of us who affirm the perpetuation of the Jewish people and Judaism are motivated not merely by a desire for self-preservation—in itself a morally legitimate motive—but by our belief that we are thereby making a contribution to humanity as a whole.

We

And

Israel

BY NOW, the books on modern Israel would veritably make up a considerable library. In sum, they deal with almost every aspect of Israeli life. Israel's fascination for tourists, Jewish as well as non-Jewish, grows from year to year, in this age of speedy travel. It is my impression that every summer, these past few years, several thousand young American Jews find their way to Israel. For all this contact, first and second hand, with Israel, I surmise that there is an unanswered question in the minds of many young people. Put simply, it is: "What are we to Israel, and what is Israel to us?"

Let us take the second half of the question first, for it is the pivotal aspect of the matter. In the first instance, Israel is the Promised Land, the land against whose varied landscape the greatest single spiritual achievement of our people in ancient times—the Bible—came into being. Here (this letter is being written in Jerusalem), the Bible receives illumination from every hill and every valley. The soil and the atmosphere are steeped in history so that, to this day, the best guide-book to Israel is the Bible. Here, the soil has been hallowed by the footprints of that galaxy of men that stretches from Abraham through the Prophets to the titans of the Talmud of the early centuries of the common era, down through all the revivals of Jewish settlement that have marked the ensuing generations.

Israel is, however, more than our past. It is inextricably bound up in Jewish thought and feeling, whose ultimate source is the prophets, with the noble messianic visions of Zion as a world spiritual center. At first glance, it seems preposterous that this tiny country, presently beset with more problems than one dares count, should ever come to play a significant role in the spiritual affairs of men. One must, nevertheless, recall that even stranger things have happened in history. Who would have dreamed that Israel would be the source of the monotheistic idea, that through its daughter religions, Christianity and Islam, it would conquer the Western World?

If this seems remote, and it does, then regard its immediate role within the sphere of Jewish life itself. Walk the streets of Jerusalem and you will hear a score of languages spoken by people with just about as many different cultural backgrounds. The physical differences between these people are enormous, to say nothing of the cultural distances that separate them. Yet they recognize one another as Jews and, for all their occasional tensions, feel joined together by this land in a common destiny.

That is true not alone of Israel. It is no less true of the Jews who live outside Israel. The interest and concern for Israel cuts across virtually all the lines that divide us into "denominations," the lines that divide us by reason of education or status, as well as the differences between American Jewry, British, French, Persian, etc. This concern, manifested by the enormous sums of money raised by World Jewry for the upbuilding of Israel, stems from both the special place this land holds in our tradition and the tremendous challenge involved in the reconstruction of a people on its ancestral soil.

How that challenge has been and is being met makes up a chapter of Jewish history that has few parallels, not alone in the annals of our long past, but in the story of mankind generally. The whole enterprise can be summed up in the phrase, "a people reborn." The unparalleled achievement has given a sense of pride to Jews throughout the world. To quote the first President of the State of Israel: "The State was not handed to us on a silver platter."

Enormous, troubling questions still remain, and will persist at least for our lifetime. What kind of social, moral, cultural and religious life will emerge here? What kind of human being will come out of this inevitable fusion of the most diverse types of Jews? What will its impact be on the Jewish people at large? These are the big questions on the horizon.

More immediately there are the pressing, urgent problems: How can this tiny country be physically secured against the threatening, implacable hostility of the surrounding Arab states? How can the level of cultural life (half of the population comes from some of the most backward areas of the world), the level of technology, be raised in a hurry? Thus, wherever one looks, close up or far-off, the people of the State of Israel are confronted with challenge. This gives life here a dynamic, seeking, questing, exciting quality. Nobody can sit back and take it easy.

Now, what has all this to do with us who live in a completely different milieu with horizons totally other than those of the Israeli landscape? What are the sources from

which our interest, concern and participation, whatever form
the latter takes, will flow? My answer is categorical: As a
Jew I am inextricably involved in the Jewish people—its
past, present and future. That, of course, in no way mini-
mizes my involvement in America. Every man has multiple
loyalties. Does my loyalty to America in anywise preclude
my concern for the fate of the rest of mankind? Or does my
devotion to, say, medicine, if I am a doctor, stand in the
way of a concern for politics? Of course, loyalties at times
do conflict with each other. If so, then I must choose on the
basis of need, truth, justice, or whatever other criteria are
applicable.

That the fate of the Jewish people is now significantly
bound with the fate of Israel, that the future of Judaism
will, in measure, at least, be determined by what happens
here to the Jewish religious tradition—these are propositions
that cannot be gainsaid.

If, then, I would have a share in helping to assure and
shape the future of the Jewish people and its religious
culture, I must have some meaningful relationship to Israel.
That can take a variety of forms. I will want, for example,
to equip myself with some knowledge of Hebrew so as to
make genuine communication possible. If it is at all possible,
I will want to spend some time here. (It is not at all
difficult for a college student to spend his Junior year here
and receive credit at his local university.) I may, as a
young professional, be willing to spend a year or two in
Israel. There is presently a crying need for all kinds of
trained technical people. (The problem of language is not
insurmountable.) There may be some young people for
whom the dynamics of Israeli society are so exciting and
fascinating as to prompt them to become a permanent part

140

of its fabric. Whatever form our participation takes, Israel ought stand high on our agenda of Jewish interest, concern and participation.

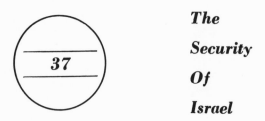

The Security Of Israel

37

AS I READ the newspapers these days, I am bewildered. Words seem to have lost their meaning and hard common-sense is smothered under blankets of meaningless verbiage. Objectives are resoundingly stated and, immediately, actions are launched that must inevitably lead to the nullification of those objectives.

In this context, consider the recent statements of our State Department and its approval of the shipping of tanks to Saudi Arabia.

In response to Israel's request for permission to buy defensive arms from our government, in the face of the eighty million dollars worth of Soviet offensive arms supplied to Egypt (jet bombers, tanks and, it is rumored, submarines), Mr. Dulles has repeatedly declared: (1) to supply arms to Israel would be to launch a dangerous armaments race in the Middle East; (2) arms are no permanent solution to the problems of the maintenance of peace and security in that area of the world; (3) the continued existence and security of Israel are part of our government's overall policy vis-a-vis the Middle East.

Let us begin with statement number 3. All Americans

142

who believe that American interests are served whenever and wherever in the world a democracy is strengthened cannot help but endorse that statement. A dictatorship is a dictatorship whether its leaders speak Russian or Arabic, and a democracy is a democracy whether its citizens speak Hebrew or English. Not one of the nine Arab countries can, even by the loosest definition of the term, qualify as a democracy. The rights guaranteed the citizens of Egypt in its new constitution were "temporarily" suspended before they went into effect. Egypt has but one legally recognized political party. And, by the way, who ever elected Nasser Prime Minister? There is only one genuine democracy in the Middle East—Israel. The existence of two wars should have taught us that when the chips are down, we cannot count on the dictatorships. (Look up the record of Spain in World War II. Also, when Rommel and his Nazis were 40 miles away from Alexandria, the Egyptian Government had not yet officially declared war against Nazi Germany. Officially, it was neutral. Actually, it was preparing to welcome the Nazis.)

What is this talk about an "arms race?" It is explained, with a show of logic, that a country with a population of 1,700,000 (Israel) cannot possibly hope to attain equality in arms with countries whose combined populations number 40 million. But Israel has no desire to match the Arabs bomber for bomber, or tank for tank. All it asks for is anti-tank guns, interceptor planes (fighter planes and not bombers), anti-submarine devices and not submarines. Besides, how can one refuse to face up to the simple question: Will the refusal of our government to sell defensive weapons to Israel act as a deterrent to the repeated Arab threats against Israel, or will such refusal rather serve to aid and abet

143

aggressive designs? To ask the question is to answer it.

Some years ago, our government took the position that Russian expansion could only be checked and deterred by their awareness that we were militarily prepared to meet and counter any aggression. We began to arm and supply our Allies with arms. We organized NATO, etc. We stockpiled military supplies. We instituted a peace-time draft for the first time in American history. Today, though there are those who urge the supplementing of this policy by such means as intensified psychological campaigns, broadened economic and social assistance to backward countries, no one yet has suggested that we disarm. If, then, we believe that a policy of strength is a major factor in deterring possible Communist aggression, why is the same policy on the part of Israel vis-a-vis the Arab countries dubbed an "arms race?" Will someone please explain the logic?

We come now to statement No. 2—"Arms are not the permanent answer to Israel's need for peace and security." Moshe Sharett, the other day, gave the telling answer to this one. That, he said, is like telling a starving man that "man does not live by bread alone." I would put it this way: Someone has suffered an accident. He is being given first aid treatment before he is taken to a hospital. Suppose a stander-by were to say: Look here, that first aid treatment is no permanent answer to the man's injury, stop giving him plasma. He needs major surgery. (Of course, he does. But unless something is done immediately, the victim of the accident may never survive.) But, it is asked, can we afford to antagonize the Arabs when they hold the oil the West (England) needs? The answer here is supplied by the military experts. In case of a showdown, the oil of the Middle East would be unavailable to the West, in any event.

144

Look at the map and see how Russia borders on Iran, next door to Saudi Arabia. The West would need a secure base for operations in that part of the world. Where would it find such a base? France and England both have their hands full now trying to hold their present bases against the inflamed nationalism of the Middle East. There is only one democracy in the area that can be counted on in a showdown—Israel. Is it, or is it not, to American interests to prevent a war in the Middle East, a war that might spark a world conflagration? Which shall we risk—a global war, or antagonizing the Arabs by deterring them from their planned and loudly trumpeted war of revenge against Israel? Anyone who can't make up his mind on that question is hopelessly befuddled.

None of this touches the underlying causes of Arab-Israeli tension. True statesmanship calls for negotiation, compromise, etc. Repeatedly, Israel has indicated its readiness to enter such negotiation without any pre-conditions. Repeatedly, the Arab countries have refused. There are points of pressure that America can exercise and should have exercised long ago to bring about such negotiations.

The issue impends, and I pray for peace. But in the meantime, it is important that all of us realize that the issue is not one alone of the security and even very existence of the State of Israel. The ultimate issue is, shall we stand idly by and see the Middle East go down the Communist drain, or shall we help secure the only bastion of democracy in the area—the State of Israel.

145

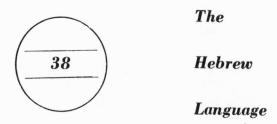

The
Hebrew
Language

IT IS more than likely that some years ago, in the course of receiving your Jewish training, you got a smattering of Hebrew. The chances are that all that you retained, besides the ability to follow a religious service in Hebrew, is a collection of stray words and phrases. (Of course, there is the miniscule minority that persisted through high school, and does possess some measure of command of the language.) It is likely that as you studied foreign languages in high school and college, some rueful questions about Hebrew occurred to you. All of them, I surmise, would add up to the suspicion that the years spent in studying Hebrew were a woeful waste. "What do I have to show for those hours and hours of study?" you ask yourself. "Besides, of what use will it ever be to me?" And then, perhaps, the final question: "Why must the service, (at least, in Conservative synagogues) be conducted primarily in Hebrew, a language unintelligible to the average worshipper?"

I am willing to grant some measure of justification to the first question. Hebrew language teaching methods in the average Jewish school could stand improvement. But, I hasten to add, that even with the very best possible method,

the average student's knowledge of the language, after
five years—the span of normal attendance at the elementary
Jewish school—would still be extremely meagre. The reasons
are not far to seek.

The Jewish school has more, much more, to teach than
language. There is Bible, Jewish history, religion, literature,
contemporary Jewish life. All of this must be crowded into
six hours per week. In addition, it must be remembered that
Hebrew is a much more difficult language than French or
Spanish. Both the latter languages have an enormous number
of cognates in English, since they belong to the same family
of languages. (Compare *mère* in French, *madre* in Spanish,
mother in English. Or, *alliance* in French, *alianza* in Spanish, alliance in English.) Hebrew belongs to an altogether
different family of languages with virtually no relationship
to English. But wait until you are a half-dozen years beyond
your language courses in high school and college, and
assuming that you have not in the interim used the languages
learned, then see how much of them you have retained.

The more important questions are really the second and
third. What actually is the purpose of studying Hebrew?
Couldn't the service, the almost exclusive domain of Hebrew
for the average Jew, be recited in English and thus offer the
worshipper intelligibility?

Consider the answer to these questions. Language is
always more than language; more than merely a tool of
communication. Language, in its depths, is the product of
a people's total life—its history, its mode of thought and
feeling, its religion. "If you would know the poet," said
Goethe, "go to the poet's country." I would rather say that
if you would know the poet, go to the poet's language. Style
is the man. No one can truly understand and grasp the

147

distinctive character of a culture without a profound, intimate grasp of its language. Translations, the very best, are like pouring old wine into new casks; inevitably, something of its bouquet is lost in the process.

Let me illustrate that truth, one which applies to all languages, to Hebrew. The Hebrew verb *yada* is translated into English "to know." But *yada*, in Hebrew, always means to have a profound intimate relationship with a person; the verb is never applied to the abstract process of cognition. In this light consider the use of the verb *yada* in two biblical verses: 1. "And Adam *yada* (knew) his wife and she conceived and bore Cain." 2. "For I (God) have known (*yada*) him (Abraham) to the end that he command his children and his household after him that they keep the way of the Lord to do righteousness and justice." In both verses, to know (*yada*) means to enter into a profound, intimate relationship, a sense of the word not to be found in English.

The examples can, of course, be multiplied almost indefinitely. They add up to this: Language is a mirror that reflects the psyche and the soul of a people more truly and deeply than almost any other known artifact. We recognize that truth when we say of someone, "he speaks another language." We intend by that phrase that the person referred to moves in an altogether different universe of discourse from our own.

Perhaps I should have offered a more commonplace example. In Hebrew, as you are aware, we do not have two different words for saying hello and goodbye. For both occasions, we use the word, *shalom*, peace. Incidentally, *shalom* does not mean simply the absence of conflict. It bears, rather, the positive meaning of harmony, fullness and wholeness.

There is, however, another and even more compelling reason for Jews to hold onto the Hebrew language with all their might. A language at its deepest level is not really translatable, because its usages carry distinct overtones. A rich patina of historic and emotional associations surround the Hebrew language. For him who knows the language, certain words and phrases, when sounded, set off powerful responses in the chambers of the heart and mind of the listener. Which phrase for the Jew, with even the slightest familiarity with the language, delivers the stronger emotional impact: "Hear, O Israel" or *Shema Yisroel?* "Exalted and magnified be His great name," or *Yitgadal v'yitkadash shmay rabbah?* With the phrase *Kol Nidre,* certain stirrings come to mind; with the phrase, "All vows," (the literal translation of *Kol Nidre*) nothing comes to the mind of the Jews.

In prayer, as in poetry, there is no precise, exact meaning of a word or phrase. One looks for precision in a scientific formula, or a legal definition, not in prayer. Tell me, if you can, to take a relatively simple example, what the following line of poetry means precisely: "She walks in beauty like the night." Prayer like poetry is essentially devotional, not intentional. It is primarily meant to create a mood rather than express a precisely defined, delineated idea. If I may offer an analogy, let me use this one: Like a flame, it is the outer glow, the perimeter that surrounds the small inner core of white light, that matters, not the latter. Even though our knowledge of Hebrew be limited in the extreme, because of its history and the associations

149

built up with it, it carries irreplaceable emotional overtones.

One final consideration. In the course of many years, I have had occasion to attend synagogues in various parts of the world. Each of them presented some strange, unfamiliar elements to an American visitor. What made me feel at home were some of the traditional, familiar prayers in Hebrew. These people, not least of all because of our common use of Hebrew, if only for the service, I recognized at once as my brethren. We shared the same devotions.

Thus, Hebrew is a precious link that still binds our people together today as it did in the past. It is still the sign of mutual recognition.

If I make no reference to the fact that Hebrew today is the daily language in the land of Israel and, thus, another link between us, it is only because the fact is too obvious and needs no elaboration.

There is a practical aspect to all this on which I would conclude. At the present stage of the development of Jewish education it is unrealistic to expect all Jews, or even most, to know Hebrew. There is however a small but growing number of young people who do have a competence in the language. But every intelligent Jew, I maintain, should know at least this much: First, the ability to follow the service in Hebrew with a fair degree of facility; secondly, a Hebrew vocabulary of the distinctive Hebrew words and phrases. To use the English version of the Hebrew is to distort their meaning. Here are a few examples:

Minyan means, of course, a quorum for a public religious service. How stilted and outlandish for a Jew to say, "I want to help make up a quorum for a public religious service," rather than, "I want to help make up a *Minyan.*" Seven days of mourning is the literal translation of *Shivah.*

A non-Jew would say, "I went to visit my friend during the seven days of mourning." A Jew says: "My friend is sitting *Shivah.*"

This, I realize, is a very minimal program of Hebrew, so small as to be dismissed by some as meaningless. There are certain vital, chemical elements which the human body requires. The amounts required are, in contrast to the need for such elements as protein and carbohydrates, truly infinitesimal. But without them the body can neither function properly nor maintain a healthy state. The irreducible amount of Hebrew knowledge here suggested, for all its minimal character, is the vital food element in the life of the Jewish people.

Juvenile
Anti-Semitism—
A
Sign
Of
The
Times

WHAT does the current rash of swastika-painting on synagogues and Jewish buildings mean? Are we facing a recrudescence of anti-Semitism? Is this, as a German Jew insisted to me today, the way Hitlerism began? Is there, therefore, genuine cause for serious concern and alarm?

I raise these questions not only because of their topicality, but because I hold a view on these matters utterly removed from that espoused, and publicly proposed, by people, including the president of a national Jewish organization whose central function is the battle against discrimination. I hold that "crying wolf" at this moment, while it will claim public attention, is no service to the Jewish people. On the contrary, if ever we should face a really serious anti-Jewish threat, one that jeopardized our rights and status, our cries of alarm and protest would be put down in the public mind as "the Jews are protesting again."

But be that as it may, what are the known facts in the present situation? Less than a year ago, carefully documented surveys by national Jewish organizations concerned with the matter reported that organized anti-Semitism in America

152

was at its lowest ebb. In fact, one could not properly speak of any organized movement. Anti-Jewish prejudice, as an opinion poll indicated, had dropped in the space of a decade and a half, to tiny proportions. (The answer came in the form of the response to the question: "Do you think any minority group forms a potential threat to the United States?") This past Monday, the *New York Times* reported on the findings of a U.N. Subcommission on Prevention of Discrimination and Protection of Minorities. The report is the result of a two-year study (30,000 words, plus separate reports on religious discrimination in 86 countries). Its conclusion: "A widespread trend exists towards equal treatment of religions and their followers."

To be sure, there are dark spots here and there. Two such instances come to mind: Soviet Russia and Germany. But even in this latter instance, one is saddened to note how those who insist on the presence of an organized anti-Semitism as a real and present danger are prone to fantastic exaggeration. Thus, on television Tuesday night, a spokesman for a national Jewish organization insisted that an anti-Semitic youth movement in Germany had 80,000 members marching around in uniforms. Compare this with this morning's *New York Times* report from Germany. *The Deutsche Bundesjugen,* the national organization of all "respectable" youth and student groups, claims five and a half million members. The right Radical group, according to the former's estimate has a total membership of 35,000 to 40,000. That makes the organized anti-Semitic youth of Germany about one-half of one percent. Thus far, all the culprits who have been caught smearing swastikas in New York—about seven have been apprehended to date— proved to be youngsters in their teens, some as young as

12 years of age, and none older than 17. Are these boys, too, part of "the international, organized conspiracy of anti-Semitism"?

If not this, what then is the real explanation of the wave of synagogue-daubing and window-breaking? I believe two elements have unconsciously joined forces, and the second is potentially a greater social danger than the first. The latter is the fact that in every society in the world, with a few horrible exceptions to be sure, there is a tiny class of hard-core anti-Semites, just as there is a hard-core of incurable alcoholics, or hobos beyond rehabilitation. A swastika, or a Jew-denouncing smear on a synagogue, is an outlet for their anti-Jewish spleen just as for some nasty minded emotionally immature youngsters scribbling "dirty" words or pictures on public toilet walls is an outlet for sexual frustration. These are the anti-Semitic masturbaters, as impotent as they are helpless. But in vast sections of today's youth there is an aimless, yet powerful anti-social urge. It would take us too far afield to explore this phenomenon and its causes. Widespread juvenile delinquency and vandalism are some of its outward expressions. Being young, these people are highly suggestible. The reports in the press, radio and television of swastika painting suggests itself as an appropriate expression for their anti-social urge.

Anti-Semitism is a foul seed that can bear the most poisonous kind of fruit. But in order to do so, it requires a certain kind of soil and nurture. The present mood of the better part of the world today—again with some striking exceptions—offers neither hospitable soil nor prospect for such nurture.

I suggest that Jewish efforts and energies have more

154

appropriate foci of attention at the moment than crying havoc at something that will pass as surely as the wave of "Rock 'n Roll" riots that last year plagued countries as remote as Japan, England and America.

Dispersal

40

And

Difference

THIS letter is being written on Purim when some old familiar words of the *Megillah* still hover over one's consciousness. In the light of contemporary eveі.ts, some of the words take on fresh pertinence. Thus, there are the words of Haman addressed to Ahasuerus in the former's bid for royal permission to destroy the Jews of Persia: "There is a certain people dispersed and scattered abroad among the nations, and their laws are different from any people, and neither do they observe the king's laws."

Clearly, two things about Jews Haman simply could not abide: their dispersal and their difference. In both respects they challenged his simplistic notion of what people ought to be and, hence, in a sense, their position threatened him. And what were these notions? People should be as he was, a Persian in Persia, no different in any respect from the average Persian. If they were not 100 percent Persian, what were they doing in Persia? They were foreigners and they didn't belong. If, on the other hand, they were Persians, why were they scattered unlike most Persians, and why did they have a set of laws and practices that both set them apart from all people and rendered them suspect in their Persian loyalty?

156

Would it be rash to generalize and say that substituting the word French, African or American for the word Persian, similar notions still predominate or, at least, have some hold over the consciousness of the mass of men? I think not. What do such slogans as "Africa for Africans," "Cuba Si, Yanquis No," "Algeria is French," or "Algeria for Algerians,"—what do these slogans betoken if not the same xenophobic narrowness and hostility that motivated Haman.

Let us go one step further and deeper. Is that not the central problem in the world today? What rivers of human blood have been set loose, what torrents of woe and disaster have been unleashed upon mankind these past few decades and for ought we know, may yet be visited upon us by reason of a mass consciousness that cannot rise to the level of a universalism sufficiently broad to accept people as they are, with all their differences.

This must be added: The typical liberal viewpoint that "all people are really substantially identical," is a willfully blind misreading of the situation and, hence, worthless as a solution to the problem. The fact of the matter is that differences between peoples, as any Sociology I or Anthropology I student ought to know, are vast and profound. Cultures, from which we draw our basic values and emotional patterns, display extraordinary differences. A Williamsburg (Brooklyn, not Virginia) Chassid, and a hillbilly from Kentucky, and a Madison Avenue executive, are all Americans but, obviously, the differences between them are monumental. I wonder what they would agree on except, perhaps, the proposition that America is a wonderful country, though the Chassid would, of course, have strong hesitations about American morals and mores. Thanks to the basic American tradition, these people, and their respec-

157

tive counterparts, can live together without periodically trying to liquidate each other. What we have achieved in America in this regard—and perhaps the greatest of our achievements, is something we ought to try to teach the rest of the world. In America, Goldberg and Ribicoff are just as American as Kennedy and Johnson.

Now, while we have written in general terms, there is an awesome aspect to this theme, one that concerns us deeply as Jews. It is this: This theme itself is a dominant mode of the historical Jewish experience. Whenever xenophobia surges upwards, and overwhelms human consciousness, no matter whether that xenophobia expresses itself in terms of a social doctrine (Communism), or religious dogma (the Middle Ages), or racialism (Nazism), or nationalism (Algeria, for example), we Jews find the ground burning under our feet.

The celebration of Purim is not only an observance of a past event. It is above all a kind of hope that the Hamans of the present and their myriads of followers (Haman had ten sons) will meet the same end as their ancient prototype.

In the marrow of my bones, I have the deepest kind of conviction that our present age of troubles is the dark and fearful prelude to a world which will witness a transformation of human consciousness, one in which being scattered and dispersed, and culturally and religiously distinctive, will be accepted as normal a human fact as the variety of the color of people's hair or eyes.

In the distant future—with growing ease of travel being what it is—I can see colonies of Americans living in Asia and Africa, just as I can see colonies of people of those continents and countries living in America, and living together in peace. A visionary Utopia? Perhaps, but the only other alternative—an endless series of "Algerias" in various parts of the world—is too dreadful to contemplate. If that vision is ever fulfilled, then we Jews will have made a singular contribution to all mankind. For have we not been these two thousand years a people dispersed among the nations, while at the same time, retaining in varying degrees, our especial distinctiveness?

41

Negro— White— Jewish Relationships

THE theme of this letter must be devoted to a painful recent episode—the recent bombings of synagogues in the South. But such are the realities of the world in which we live. Besides, you, like all Jews, must surely have been profoundly shocked by the news that a synagogue in Atlanta, one in Peoria and several others, earlier in the year, had been the targets of bombs.

The episode itself and the attendant circumstances have been amply described in the press. To these descriptions I have nothing to add. It is the meaning of these events that concerns me.

What is the context in which these episodes must be placed? As I see it, the bombing of synagogues, threatening anonymous telephone calls to rabbis, etc. . . . ., are the side reaction of the current struggle for desegregation *and not the symptoms of a genuine flare-up of anti-Semitism.* At first glance, this might seem far-fetched, but such are the complexities and hidden interrelationships of apparently remote social forces, that Negro-White tension can have distinct repercussions on the Jewish situation. Let us trace out this hidden yet very real relationship.

160

There is no area in the country where Jewish-Gentile relationships are stronger and closer than in the South. (To be sure, this involvement does not go beyond 6:00 P.M. In the evening there is very little if any social relationship between Jews and Gentiles, visiting back and forth, going to the same country club, etc.) But with this single limitation, Jewish-Gentile relationships are close in business and community life. There are, for example, more Jewish mayors and important city government officials in the South per capita Jewish population than there are in the North. So, the Jewish position in the South may be described as that of a respected minority, high on the side of community acceptance, but socially apart.

Now, the most bitter, fanatical, anti-Negro element in the South comes from the latter's lowest white social stratum—the "poor white," the frustrated little people, the proletariat, some of the lower middle class. As always, these elements must have a scapegoat, as we say in Yiddish—a *kapporeh*—on whom to vent their frustration and towards whom they can feel superior. When the Negro begins to move in a positive way towards equality, as they have in recent years, these elements feel themselves threatened. Their paranoia-ridden souls are enlarged and sustained when they make themselves the defenders of such principles(?) as Gentile-White supremacy. The threat of desegregation throws them into a frenzy since it seems to rob them of their chief psychological prop—their sense of superiority. Hence, these people are prepared to go to any lengths to stave off segregation—somethings every intelligent Southerner knows is as inevitable as tomorrow's sunrise. This rising pent-up force must find its outlet. What better target than the big, beautiful synagogue, symbol of the Jew's having arrived.

Besides, socially and economically, the Jew—the partial outsider—stands head and shoulders above the poor native White. Anti-Negro and Anti-Jew is part of a single syndrome. Fortunately, these elements—certainly its activist sector—are relatively infinitesimal in number. The vast, overwhelming majority of the Southern community harbors a respectful and friendly attitude towards Jews. (Within hours after the Atlanta synagogue was bombed, a half-dozen churches offered their facilities to the congregation. Non-Jews gathered a substantial sum of money as a reward to anyone giving information leading to the apprehension of the culprits.)

One wishes the discussion could be closed on this optimistic, promising note. But a sense for the realities bids us to look a bit farther and deeper. The liberal elements in the South prepared to advance the cause of complete integration are pitifully few and silent. The moderate elements are willing to accept limited integration, grudgingly, slowly, and as the lesser of two evils, the other being the closing of the public schools. The majority are prepared to fight it tooth and nail.

What should be the attitude of the Southern Jew in this situation? Prudence would command silence on the part of a minority community. But moral honesty and courage—and the Jewish tradition—commands that Jews speak up in behalf of right and justice. We, certainly, of all people, who have known the worst forms of segregation and social exclusions, should lift one voice on behalf of human rights. To be sure, such a stand will not win us friends, except perhaps among the Negroes. On the contrary, it may severely shake the whole Jewish-Gentile relationship in the South for a while. But what, let us recall, do we think of the Germans who during the Hitler period looked the other way and pretended not to see the hurt and shame being visited on the Jew? Finally, it is the part of wisdom to remember that some day the Negro will win this fight. Where will we then be able to hide our cowardly neutrality?

Of course, we in the North do not come into this fight with clean hands. There are a hundred and one forms of anti-Negro discrimination among us. It is time all of us, North and South, began to put our house in order.

Somehow, history has a habit of putting us Jews on the firing line where the battles for human dignity, freedom and equality are being fought. The battle line extends from the Middle East to Atlanta to Little Rock and to everybody's home town.

**Equality
And
Difference—
Reflections
On
Integration**

THERE are two Americas. One is white; the other is black. For all its conspicuousness, that is really the least of the differences. Consider some of them.

White America straddles the whole economic, educational and moral scale. Black America is preponderantly bunched pretty near the bottom of each of these scales. So wide are the contrasts that it is difficult to believe that these two communities inhabit the same country, are segments of the same society and, in community after community across the country, live within a few blocks of each other.

That, in brief, is the background of the present agonizing struggle, a struggle which, I venture to say, will go on and on through at least the lifetime of the present college generation.

It goes without saying, of course, that you who read this are on the side of the angels and that wherever you can, you raise your voice in behalf of human dignity and justice. But precisely because you believe that Negroes should not be treated as second-class citizens nor, least of all, as second-class human beings, a certain realism is called for.

Hopefully, the Civil Rights legislation now before Congress will be enacted into law. Will that legislation fundamentally alter the situation I have described in the first paragraph of this letter? Certainly not. Neither the miles of squalid slums in the Northern cities, nor the shanties in the Southern cities, will vanish when President Kennedy puts his signature to the Civil Rights Bill. The mass of unskilled Negro labor will be just where it is now. The number of Negro college students will not rise precipitously overnight. All that will have been done—and it is the first tremendous step—is the prevention of further psychological wounds inflicted on Negroes by American society, day after day. That, and something else! The conditions will have been set for the long, slow, painful climb for the mass of American Negroes out of poverty, ignorance and squalor—social and moral. That climb will take decades, perhaps several generations. A hundred years ago, Lincoln emancipated the Negroes. It may take the Negroes another hundred years to emancipate themselves. Negro frustration now has a legimate target. But once legal equality has been established the even more difficult process will have to begin. What if Negroes are freely admitted to hotels, restaurants, colleges, etc., if so pitifully few can either afford to stay at the hotels or have the desire to go to college?

Perhaps enough has been said to indicate that the real Negro problem will begin once legal equality will have been attained. So much on the side of realism on the Negro problem.

But there is another aspect to the question to which relatively little thought has been given. One hears from many quarters—"What difference should the color of a man's skin make? Are not all people essentially the same?" The answer to the first question is that the color of a man's

165

skin should make no difference as far as his rights, privileges and opportunities are concerned. In a word, all men are, or should be equal. But—and this is the nub of the matter— equal does not mean identical, nor does it mean sameness. Men are diverse, societies are varied and have their own attitudes and values, tastes and sensibilities. "There is not much difference between one man and the next," said William James. Then he went on to say, "But what there is, is mighty important."

I should think that a Negro mind and spirit, that a Negro consciousness of the world, is not the same as that of, say, a white Protestant, or an Irish Catholic, or an American Jew of East European background.

These considerations, of course, go far beyond the immediate context of the problem of the Negro. If they are valid, and I believe they are, then they have significance for us as Jews. A hundred and fifty years ago, and more, when Jews in Western Europe were fighting for civil rights, some made that egregious error of basing their claims for equality on the proposition that Jews were essentially no different from Germans or Frenchmen. Perhaps they really meant it. But, history proved they were tragically mistaken. It would be a tragic denouement of the present struggle for equal rights for Negroes if the Negro on the morrow of the successful culmination of that struggle, would try to make himself over in the image of the white man, instead of maintaining and fostering what is unique and valuable in his own Negro heritage.

166

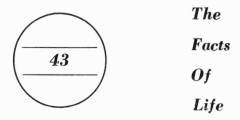

The

Facts

Of

Life

43

KING SOLOMON who in our tradition is known as the wisest of all men did not hesitate to confess, in a moment of candor, that there were four things that were beyond his understanding. The climactic one in his series of four mysteries and, hence, presumably the most incomprehensible is, "The way of a man with a maid." Admittedly, then, love and sex baffled him.

We, in this post-Freudian generation, are prone to smile condescendingly at this admission of ignorance on the part of an ancient man reputedly exceedingly wise. Who today does not presumably know the facts of sex and love, and their inter-relationship? Indeed, modern people decry and deny the whole notion that there is anything at all mysterious about sex and love. Blunt outspokenness, to the point of casualness, characterizes the contemporary novel and play on this score. For that matter, even the daily newspaper (witness the Profumo scandal) has lost its one-time reticence on the subject. The manifestations of this attitude are both too numerous and too blatant to require enumeration.

What attitude does this "modern" treatment of sex and love bespeak? What is its underlying, if unspoken, axiom?

It is, I believe, the notion that sex is nothing more and nothing less than a biological urge, no more mysterious and no more significant than, say, human thirst. Indeed, a character in a recent novel characterizes the sex act as just that: "Nothing more than a drink of water."

Two fields of study have directly and indirectly made their contribution to the formation of this attitude. Freudianism, with its pan-sexual theories, is largely responsible for the notion that love is really a kind of washed out sex, that the emotions of tenderness and affection are basically sexual in origin. Anthropology, on the other hand, has studied primitive societies (*Coming of Age in Samoa*) and seems to point to the conclusion that the lack of sexual repression in these uncivilized societies somehow leads to a free and easy naturalness unknown to civilized people.

These theories aside for the moment, the implications of the attitude described above are obvious and they too, truth to tell, are all around us. For if sex is just that, and nothing more—the satisfaction of a biological need—then clearly, the traditional standards of sex morality, such as pre-marital chastity, have received a mortal blow.

To return to the anthropologists: The point is precisely that 20th century civilized man is not growing up in a stone-age Samoa. To the uncivilized man, sex is exactly what some contemporary sophisticates say it is—nothing more than a biological urge. The primitive man has yet to relate his sexual urge to such sentiments as tenderness, affection and love. For him, any sex object will do. It was in the long slow climb to civilization that man learned to relate his sex urge with the psychological needs of his ego, his need to be loved, his need to be supremely important to a member of the opposite sex, and the tenderness and affection that these engender. How this conjunction came about, no one really knows but clearly, for civilized people, sex is more than its purely physical aspect. Involving the deepest layers of the ego, it involves the total personality and not simply the physiological system. To attempt to divorce the two now is, to put it plainly, to revert to the stage of pre-civilization. (But then, is this the only area in which modern man with his ferocious violence appears to threaten reversion to barbarism?)

Grant, then, as I believe one must as civilized human beings, that the conjunction between sex and the ego, once having been made, to disassociate them is not alone a reversion to primitivism, it is the beginning of the disintegration of the personality. In this connection, I suggest that you turn to the Bible and read one of the most insightful stories about sex ever written. I have reference to the story of Amnon and Tamar. (You will find it in the Second Book of Samuel, chapter 13, verses 1-20.) Note, in verse 15, the words: "For the hatred wherewith he hated her was greater than the love wherewith he had loved her." Physical desire without love—sheer sex—leads to revulsion in a truly civilized human being. For, in the latter, sex certainly involves the total person. If that be so, it follows that sexual fulfillment is in order, and is morally and psychologically significant where there is a total, mutual, permanent commitment of the self. In a word, in the state of marriage.

But what of the mystery of sex with which we began our reflection? It turns out to be, does it not, nothing less than part of the mystery of the total personality of the self. And the latter, I insist, is ultimately a mystery, never totally disclosed to anyone. Sex brings us to a deeper awareness of another person—hence the Bible uses the verb "to know," as a metaphor for sexual communion. ("And Adam knew his wife Eve.") But the total person forever eludes us.

I cannot close this letter without sounding one more note. (No one is more aware than I that there are vast, involved aspects of the psychology of sex and love which I have not even touched on. But even this single insight I offer should be enough to scotch the notion that "sex is nothing more than . . ." And that everybody really knows the "facts of life.") Judaism never regarded marriage and sex, as did Christianity, as a concession to the weakness of the flesh. It never regarded chastity as a holy ideal meant for the spiritually elect. On the contrary, man's natural, moral and spiritual state, Judaism has always consistently taught, is the state of matrimony. In Judaism, sex is neither a salacious joke, a casual drink of water, or a concession to importunate human desires. It is a significant aspect of life through which human fulfillment is reached, and when it involves the total personality, it engages that self whose mystery ultimately reflects the mystery of God, its Creator.

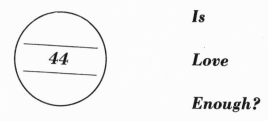

Is

Love

Enough?

THIS letter is the first in a series of three on the theme of Love, Sex and Marriage. I am moved to discuss this theme with you and to respond to any questions you might have on the position I maintain.

We are now in the wake of a tremendous upheaval. To be more accurate, one might say it is one part of upheaval, and two parts confusion. Early (college) marriage is an obvious manifestation of this upheaval. A generation ago it was a rare young man who married before he had fairly started on his career. What has brought about this startling change, and is it one that we ought welcome? (My answer to the latter question will become apparent in the course of this series of letters.)

I begin by challenging the truth of what can be called the romantic love myth of our culture. It is assumed, and the assumption forms the basis for so much of the literature, movies and TV programs of our day that love, a mysterious passion, is the solid, enduring base for marriage. The fact that two young people love each other makes them suitable partners in marriage, and virtually guarantees that theirs will be a happy, fulfilling marriage.

No notion is more fallacious or potentially more destructive of marriage. The plain truth is that the success or failure of marriage is not dependent on romantic love. A moment's reflection should make that clear. If the notion were true then, since virtually all young people enter marriage romantically in love with each other, why do so many marriages end in separation and divorce? Moreover, we know of other cultures, past and present, in which romantic love is not a factor, and yet marriages stand up at least as well, if not better than ours.

Romantic love assumes that "love conquers all," and that it is an unfailing bridge over all the difficulties, problems and objective differences between two young people. By its very nature, romantic love is the antithesis of married love. Romantic lovers pursue each other. In marriage, two people have each other. Romantic love thrives on obstacles, enforced separations, etc. Married love thrives on sharing, and a minimum of such obstacles. Romantic love tends towards mutual idealization. ("He or she," romantic lovers say, "is my ideal.") Married love faces and accepts the realities of the personality and character of the marriage partner.

Nor do we need to theorize on the subject. Scores of factual studies have indicated with irrefutable unanimity, that where two young people possess fairly similar social, educational and religious backgrounds the prospects for a successful marriage are enormously better than where these factors are dismissed as irrelevant.

Does all this mean that love per se is nothing more than an aberration of one's youth? Not at all. There is such a thing as real, mature love, but it is nothing like what is celebrated in current novels, movies and popular songs. You love a person if his well-being, his growth toward his great-

172

est potential in all facets of his personality, matters to you as much as your own. Real love is mutual. Only two people who can accept themselves can give acceptance and love to others. Real love is not all absorbing. It never makes a person less effective. Real love is congeniality and helps us to be our real selves.

The key to mature love is maturity. So the essential question one must put to oneself before entering a permanent liaison is: "Have I reached a relative maturity, a stability of emotional growth, or am I just romantically in love? Have I reached the point in my maturation where I am ready to make a permanent decision, or am I being swept along on a tide of feeling that refuses to reckon with the realities?" In the answer to that question, you have my attitude towards early marriages. Some people are mature at twenty and some will never grow up if they live to be a hundred and twenty.

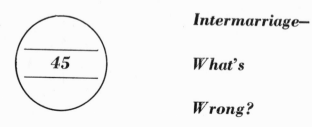

Intermarriage—

What's

Wrong?

45

FOLLOWING last month's discussion of love, this letter should logically deal with marriage. Instead, it is devoted to the theme of Inter-Marriage. Why? Because I am convinced that the tendencies that make marriage outside the faith a likely possibility are already present in the individual long before he or she even begins to seriously contemplate marriage. Further, the problems it poses both to the individual and the Jewish people can never be resolved, they can only be prevented. Like the common cold, no one has yet discovered a real cure for it; it can only be prevented. Hence, on both counts, some hard thinking on inter-marriage is called for long before a Jewish young man or woman is emotionally involved with a non-Jew, not after. Let me explicate this last statement, based on my thirty years of experience. And then, we will come back to what I have called the "tendencies" towards inter-marriage.

Over the years, distraught parents have repeatedly appealed to me to dissuade a son or daughter from marrying outside the faith. I have long since given up that hopeless, impossible task. Not that the arguments against inter-marriage are weak, and will not stand up under critical

scrutiny. On the contrary, the arguments are logically irresistible. Consider them briefly.

Statistical evidence, gathered by non-Jewish researchers,
who certainly have no axe to grind, indicate conclusively
that the ratio of broken homes, divorce, separation, aban-
donment, in an inter-married household, were about three
to one, as against families where both husband and wife are
of the same religious background. In a word, he who inter-
marries runs an enormously larger risk of coming to grief
in his married life than he who marries within the fold.
Again, every intermarriage, more likely than not, represents
a distinct loss to Judaism and the Jewish people. (A recent
study in Washington, D.C. reveals that 70 percent of the
children of inter-married Jewish-Christian couples are being
reared as Christians.) Hence, in a very real sense, a decision to marry outside the faith is an act of betrayal of
Judaism and our people.

Finally, I have yet to meet Jewish parents who can look
upon a son's or daughter's inter-marriage with equanimity.
Does one have the right to achieve what one deems to be
one's own happiness at the cost of the anguish and heart-
break of one's own parents? Well, I might go on and pile
up the arguments, rational and moral against inter-marriage.
But since when can a young man or woman, deeply in love,
be reached, let alone be persuaded, by rational argument?
Love, as we have seen in our previous discussion, is in its
very nature non-rational and thrives on non-rationality. Who
ever argued or reasoned himself or herself "into" love or
"out of" love? One falls in love, and in that state, to
reason with a person in love is tantamount to trying to talk
sense to someone who is dead drunk. (The poets speak of
love as a kind of intoxication.) In all my years—I have

175

long since given up trying— I have never dissuaded any-one who was already deeply emotionally involved with a non-Jew to break off that relationship. In that sense, I say that inter-marriage cannot be cured. One can only be im-munized against it, so to speak, and, I ought add at once, no immunization can ever be guaranteed.

This brings us to the "tendencies" of which I spoke above. There are those, not too many but enough, who carry within themselves an unconscious, but decided, proclivity towards inter-marriage. Young people who come from families marked by excessive wrangling between parents are likely to choose as their life partner someone as different from their own parents as possible. Young people whose relationship to their own parents is marked by strong re-jection and hostility are likely to choose a non-Jewish mate as a final act of defiance. Then, of course, there are those who find their Jewish identity irksome. What better pass-port to Gentile identity and status than a non-Jewish mate?

In addition to these tendencies, largely psychological and unconscious, I would add one's own immediate social situation. Young people who are thrown together by cir-cumstance: attending the same class, working in the same office—can be attracted to each other. One, two, three dates together, and a growing emotional rapport can soon bring these to the point where their initial scruples against inter-marriage begin to wear thin and, then, vanish. Two-thirds of the Jews who inter-marry, as a recent book in-dicates (*Jewish-Gentile Courtsnips*, by John Mayer), started out with strong convictions against marrying outside the faith. "If someone had told me five years ago, that I would marry a non-Jew, I would have said that he was crazy." That is not an atypical statement.

What does all this mean in practical, everyday terms? If you share the basic commitment—and I assume that you do—that you want Judaism and the Jewish people to continue in the world, then you must determine to marry within the fold. But this abstract determination is meaningless, as we have seen, unless you are prepared to make a reality of it. How? Very simply. Your social life, i.e. dates, ought be restricted to members of the Jewish faith. Do I hear someone retorting: bigotry, intolerance, segregation? I reply: Since when is it a mark of intolerance to want to (1) assure oneself, as far as one can, that the risks of unhappiness in marriage are minimized; (2) assure the perpetuation of a people and a religion with a three-thousand year old history not without its universal significance and nobility?

I have said above there is no perfect immunization against inter-marriage. Where it is inevitable, then the Jewish partner has a duty to seek to bring the non-Jewish partner into the Jewish fold, especially where the latter has no particular strong roots in his or her own religious community. People who sincerely accept Judaism we regard as full and complete Jews. Is such persuasion—where persuasion is necessary—fair? There is no easy answer. But that a household should have one religious allegiance, not two, goes without saying. "A house divided against itself cannot stand."

The time to talk about inter-marriage, take one's stand and live one's life accordingly, is *now*, when the prospect of marriage is not immediate. I invite you to do so by reading this letter carefully and discussing it with your friends.

177

**Is
Early
Marriage
For
You?**

ONE OF the silent, important revolutions taking place in our time in American society is the precipitate drop in the age at which young people marry. Strange as it may sound, to my generation, only three decades ago, a married college student, undergraduate or graduate, was a very rare phenomenon. Today, virtually every university of any size provides dormitory facilities for married students.

Whatever the reasons for this dramatic change, and sociologists have attempted to explore them, the fact of relatively early (student) marriage inevitably raises some important problems upon whose successful resolution the happiness and stability of an increasingly large number of people hinge. The question of whether or not early marriage is desirable does not presently concern me. I accept it as a fact. However, the consequences that flow from that fact do concern me. And perhaps, on the basis of our airing of these consequences you can come to your own decision whether or not student marriage is for you.

The initial problem, as I see it, is that young people in their choice of a mate are prone to fail to give proper weight to important factors that ought to enter in the making of such choice. I have reference to such factors as a reasonable similarity of background, an approximate similarity of tastes, a mutual religious consensus. Now, it is notoriously true that young people are inclined to act on the proposition, as if it were unquestionable truth, that love conquers all or, the even more fallacious notion, that opposites attract. (They may occasionally attract, but will they hold?) The love emotion in its powerful intensity can cause a young person to blithely disregard the very elements that have been empirically demonstrated again and again, to be determinative of a durable, happy marriage. The number of broken marriages among those who have married at an early age is extraordinarily high. The chances are great that there are some within the circle of your own acquaintances.

But granting that one has made a marriage choice where all the factors point for success, the problems are not done with. The truth is that marriage, like most human ventures, solves some problems for the people involved, but at the same time creates others.

The first few years of marriage, generally speaking, are the most difficult. Once these years have been weathered, the stability and satisfaction a marriage yields should increase as the years go on. Let me indicate some of the shoals that have to be navigated.

Of primary importance is the recognition and understanding that the romantic love that brought one to one's mate is not enough to sustain marriage. Several basic adjustments to reality are required. In the first instance, it is only in marriage that one discovers the actual contours of the character and temperament of one's mate. (Before marriage, two young people see each other through a romantic haze; hence, the saying, "love is blind.") More than once, I have

179

heard young married people say, in bitter disillusionment, he or she is not the same person I married. Obviously, the statement is egregiously false. Marriage does not change one's basic cast of character or personality, it merely reveals it to one's mate for the first time.

This is the first challenge of marriage, learning to fully accept and affirm each other just as one is. Remember, that if marriage brings genuine discovery of one's mate, it also brings self-revelation. What is true on the physical level is true on the spiritual and psychological level.

In romantic courtship, one seeks to look as physically attractive as possible. Who would go out on an important date unshaven? Or what girl does not prepare for such occasions with a frenetic meticulousness as to dress, hair, face, etc. Then, after marriage, two people see each other in esthetic disarray, without the aid of careful grooming. They see each other's real being in much the same way.

It takes some insight and understanding to realize that though it may be launched in a romantic blaze, marriage is sustained and propelled not so much by that initial impulse, but by acts, words and gestures in the context of everyday life, and all its situations, petty or significant.

I wrote above of mutual acceptance and affirmation as the basis of a realistic grasp of one another's true being. The terms acceptance and affirmation must be explicated. The greatest single psychological need of the individual is the sense that he or she is of supreme importance to the person one regards as supremely important in one's life. In marriage, mutual acceptance and affirmation are not, as they may be in other spheres, a one-time act. Married people, even happily married people, ask each other, over

180

and over again, "do you love me," and eagerly await an affirmative answer. This is the blood-stream of marriage.

Of course, verbal articulations of acceptance and affirmation are not enough. A deed intended to make one's mate feel that he or she is supremely precious is even more effective than words, though the latter are not to be discounted. One's whole stance and posture, one's words, deeds, gestures, even tone of voice, must, in effect be saying to one's mate: "You are the most important person in the world to me."

I am not suggesting that two people in order to be happy, joyful and content in marriage must live in a constant state of amorous tension with each other. Not at all. I do, however, insist that they must face each other, and relate to each other, on a unique level of mutual concern, appreciation and responsiveness. It is into these that romantic love must flower, if marriage is not to degenerate into either boredom or quiet desperation.

Even if this atmosphere has been created by two people, occasions can and do arise, in the context of daily life, in which conflict, misunderstanding and tension destroy or at least temporarily suspend their mutual attitude. Only human beings, not angels, marry. And who, occasionally, is not guilty of thoughtlessness or selfishness, or any one of the traits that make up our shadow side? On such occasions, marriage is tested. The test can be passed successfully only if people have the maturity to communicate in candor, and reach each other above the barricades of anger and hurt pride that make communication so difficult in such moments. Marriages do not explode instantaneously; they disintegrate slowly. Every such situation which is not talked out in

181

mutual understanding, followed by an even deeper acceptance and affirmation, is a corroding acid in what so many married people call a drifting apart.

This is the essential outline of what can make a good marriage to begin with, and what is needed to make it grow more durable and deeply satisfying. A failure to grasp it and apply it is certain to result either in a broken marriage or, what is just as bad, a state of resignation that leads to quiet desperation.

The failure of so many young marriages is simply the reflection of the not unexpected fact that many, if not most young people, have not as yet ripened emotionally. If you have any doubts on that score, you would be well advised to wait.

47

Silence
At
A
Time
Like
This!

THERE is a passage in the *Megillah* which we read this past Saturday night in observance of Purim, that keeps haunting me. Let me put it in its proper context. Mordecai has received word that Haman has obtained royal consent to slay the Jews of Persia. Only a personal appeal to the king can suspend the decree. And only one person can make that plea—Esther. But what is Esther to do? For she knows the law and practice of ancient Persia, that anyone who comes unbidden into the presence of the king may summarily be executed. This, in effect, is the message she sends to Mordecai when the latter implores her to go to the king and stand in the breach. To which Mordecai replies: "If thou be silent at a time like this . . . then thou and all thine house will perish. Do not imagine that you alone, being in the king's house, will escape of all the Jews."

The passage that seems to leap across the centuries, and knock at all our doors is: "If thou be silent at a time like this." For there are situations in all our lives, and in our society generally, that do seem to cry out to us: "If thou be silent at a time like this." And yet there are few, if any, who dare to speak.

Indeed, the common philosophy of our age is, "Don't stick out your neck. Why be the fall guy?" The man who succeeds is the one who can make friends and influence people. Speaking up for unpopular causes and ideas, daring to say no when everyone says yes, calling into question the tastes and standards of the market place, will win you no friends and give you such social B.O. that even your best friends won't tell you. So with the tacit philosophy of "play it safe," it is no wonder that the average college student today is simply inarticulate on social and moral problems. Values in life, outside of "a good time now and a good career later," appear to be as remote from the student's sphere of real interest as the rocket Pioneer V is at the moment from the earth (a half million miles).

Now it seems to me that the real business of education, aside from vocational or professional training, is the development of a set of values to which one is committed, and for which one is prepared to speak up, be the risks what they may. Let me concretize this by two examples, one negative, and one affirmative.

Not too long ago, an investigation revealed that some students at various universities were getting their term papers and even M.A. and Ph.D. dissertations, ghost written at a price, by one or another agency engaged in the business. When payola moves into academic halls where the lamp of knowledge and the pursuit of truth are supposed to be the high ideals, then one has good cause for throwing up one's hands in despair for such society. In five, ten, or fifteen years, these people will be occupying important positions in the professional and business world. What hope is there for a society if its ablest, best informed minds, have

184

no compunctions about playing fast and loose with truth. Let me make it more specific. Would a fraternity expel a member if it discovered that he cheated at exams or passed off as his own, someone else's paper? I say, and I hope I am mistaken, but I think the answer is no.

Now for the affirmative illustration. Anyone seriously concerned with religion on the campus is regarded, so we surmise, as somewhat queer. Religious students find themselves embarrassed and tongue-tied when it comes to flatly declaring how important they feel religion is. Students who believe and practise pre-marital chastity become apologetic in the presence of those who vaunt their freedom.

Actually, no one yet has made out a convincing theory for either irreligion or pre-marital promiscuity. The profoundest minds and the noblest spirits of the race have invariably been deeply concerned with the issues of religion. All experience indicates, aside from the irrefragable moral considerations involved, that promiscuity is destructive of character and adds immeasurably to the hazards of marriage.

There is no lack of situations where we dare not be silent. There are grave social issues, there are international problems fraught with "portentous explosive issues," on which we dare not be silent.

But to speak out requires courage. And courage comes ultimately from faith in what we deem to be truth and justice and wisdom. If education be not intended to integrate these into the fiber of our minds and souls, then I know not what it is for.

One final word: The glory of our people are the prophets, men who refused to be silent, when being silent meant playing it safe. There is a saying in the Talmud: "The people of Israel, if they are not prophets, then they are the children of prophets." The sound of some prophetic thunder would be heavenly music.

"When In Rome..."

OVER the year, I have succumbed to a rather strange mental habit. Whenever, in my reading, I come across a pungent, meaningful phrase or dictum in traditional Jewish literature, I pause and ask myself: What is its non-Jewish equivalent? I ransack my mind and, occasionally, the encyclopedias of quotations, beginning with Bartlett, then going on to the French, German, etc. I want to share with you, in this letter, the fruits of one such comparative study.

The other day, re-reading the *Ethics of the Fathers* (*Pirke Avot*, a treatise of the Mishnah, edited ca. 200 C.E.), I stopped at this saying of Hillel's: "In a place where no one is acting as a man should, strive to be a man." Try as I would, I could find no popular saying quite like it in the literature of folk expression. Indeed, the only thing I came up with is the familiar, "When in Rome, do as the Romans," an attitude that stands antipodally opposed to Hillel's. Latterly, I have been meditating on the contrast.

Obviously, Hillel's saying is pregnant with challenge and moral lift. The other is self-justification and, in a sense, almost a factual statement, a report of how most men act when they find themselves in "Rome." Implied in both is the realization that our environment does wield a massive influence on our conduct. Indeed, this fact has, in some circles, been turned into a philosophy that would tell us that morals are nothing more than the mores of a group. Hence, there are really no moral imperatives. Better or worse, in this connection, means compliance with, or deviation from, local moral standards and nothing more. Two observations are in order here.

Man alone, in distinction to all other creatures, can react to the environment in three contrasting ways; he can adapt himself to it, he can change it (as we do constantly with our physical environment), or he can transcend it, rise superior to it. Swamps breed mosquitos. But out of the same poverty-stricken slums from which society's anti-social elements emerge, there has come, time and again, some of our most distinguished citizens, people who transcend their environment.

Yet another observation is called for on this equating of morals with mores. By this token, a German who promptly adapted himself to the "standard" and practices of Nazi culture, acted morally; a German who defied them at great personal risk—and there were a few such—acted immorally! On some other occasion, we might examine the theories of the moral relativists more fully. In the meantime, I would urge a strong measure of skepticism of the theory, often propounded in courses in sociology and anthropology, that man is nothing more than the product of his environment, and that adaptation to it is the *summum bonum*.

Indeed, man must resist his environment as much as he must adapt to it. All of us, in this age of growing collectivism, are threatened with being swallowed up in the faceless, anonymous mass and becoming less than individuals. More and more, we Americans are becoming other-directed people, to use David Reisman's apt phrase. Our goals, standards, tastes and ideas do not spring from any inner sources of our own, but are borrowed from our peer-groups. In a sense, "when in Rome, do as the Romans," threatens to become our national philosophy. Of one thing we may be sure: That way lies the destruction of that which is most precious in the world—the individual self.

Besides, what is the moral life, anyhow? Is it merely conforming to the moral code, and observing the conventional, "thou shalt nots?" Is a man who does not steal, lie etc., truly a moral person? Not by the standards of Judaism. More, much more, is required. The ethical life demands effort, self-sacrifice, the ability on occasion, to forego one's own self-interests, on behalf of others. In other words, morality is challenge, not conformity; the kind of challenge implied in Hillel's dictum.

Where, in our society, is such challenge to be found? I think it is the business of all of us to find it in our own individual lives. Whether we be students or are engaged in our careers, there are situations and opportunities where we can exercise the first requisites of the moral life—a measure of self-sacrifice. I know, for example, of a school where the Jewish students have voluntarily assessed themselves a dollar a week as a contribution to Israel. Out of the average student's budget, that represents something of a sacrifice. I think, too, in this connection of the coming summer. There must be scores of settlement house summer camps for underprivileged children in need of college people to serve as counsellors at very moderate salaries. Someone who took such a job in preference to a well-paid job in a private camp would be performing a truly ethical act. That would be fulfillment of Hillel's injunction. But whatever the nature of the act, the spirit of Jewish ethics calls for moral effort, not merely compliance with the mores of our times.

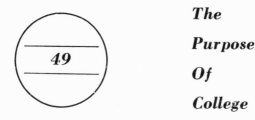

The Purpose Of College

I WOULD like to begin this letter by posing a question. What do you hope to get out of college? Obviously, a variety of answers is possible, some of them complementary, others mutually exclusive. One answer might be, preparation for a career; another, four pleasant years; still a third, widened mental horizons. Thus, the answers might run on and on and include such candid replies as, "Meet interesting people of the opposite sex." The cynic might say with the late Lincoln Steffens, "It's worth going to college to find out what you can't get at college."

Whatever the immediate aim, worthy or trifling, may I suggest another; one, that to me, at least, is indispensable. Indeed, unless it is fulfilled in some measure, your four years at college whatever else they may give you, will have failed you. Here it is: College should give you a set of values.

What are values? Values are the criteria of conduct, experience and belief. If in these three areas, conduct, experience and belief, a college graduate is undistinguishable from someone who has not spent four years at a school of higher learning, what actually has a college education done for him as a human being besides preparing him to earn a living? If his moral standards are no better—his sense of integrity, for example, no more profound; his arc of meaningful experiences—the things he appreciates—no wider or no more refined; his beliefs no broader and deeper; if, in all these spheres the college graduate cannot see farther and clearer than the average man, of what earthly good are history, science, literature, etc?

Obviously, I do not subscribe to the maxim "Knowledge for the sake of knowledge," any more than I subscribe to the slogan, "Art for art's sake." That may serve the purpose of television quiz programs. So you know the names of King Henry VIII's five wives—so what! In Jewish thinking, the study of Torah was for the purpose of conduct, and utlimately, conduct depends on experience and belief.

But you ask, what has Bio 1, or History 27, or English 73, got to do with life, my life, with conduct, experience and belief? A fair question. The answer is that all human knowledge is not only interrelated but is related to the real ever-present problems of human life, for it helps us understand the processes of life—past and present.

Let me now, by way of illustration, examine the area of belief. The infinite complexity of the physical world, its unfathomable inter-relationships, the complex structure of the smallest particle of matter; in other words, the vistas opened up by science, indicate that no small, childlike concept of God as a benevolent old gentleman will do. Far from diminishing God, modern physical science, it seems to me, requires one who has some glimpse of its discoveries, to conceive of the source of all being in terms of an awesome majesty that transcends the human grasp.

Now, of course, I am aware that there are those who say

192

that science renders God remote, if not completely unnecessary. Laplace, the 18th century astronomer, is reported to have said to Napoleon, "Sire, I have swept the heavens with my telescope and can find no trace of God." Obviously, Laplace was looking for an old gentleman sitting on a throne. Instead, he ought have asked himself a series of simple questions: If there be no intelligence, no rationality, no will in the universe, how did these qualities ever emerge in man, who, after all, has himself emerged out of the processes of life? If there be no consciousness in the world, where did human consciousness come from? Indeed, the old Latin maxim still holds: *Ex nihil nihil fit.* (Out of nothing, nothing can be made.) What Laplace needed, and, what I suspect many of us need, is a broader, deeper concept of God.

Nor do I particularly recommend starting by contemplating the physical world. Begin by contemplating yourself and your human relationships. What makes human society possible? The fact of reason and speech! Through these two avenues we can communicate with one another. They make possible the faith in the coming into being of a single humanity, able to transcend the differences that history and culture have developed, and will continue to develop. But reason and speech are not simply human products. (No one yet has been able to find the bridge from animal instinct to human reason or from animal sounds to human speech. In order for man to reason, his fellowman must already have been susceptible to the persuasiveness of reason. In order for man to speak, someone must already have been able to understand speech.) Thus, reason and speech are as much a gift as they are a human product. But since they are universal, the giver of the gift must be universal—he

193

must possess purpose in the giving of the gift. In other words, He must be God. The purpose? The possibility for man to achieve universal solidarity.

Once you have grasped this, you have gotten hold of a basic principle of Jewish faith. The faith expressed in the words of our prayer on Rosh Hashanah: "That men may unite to form one band to do Thy will with a perfect heart."

The example I have offered of a growth and depth in our idea of God is but an illustration of what ought take place, as a result of a college education in all aspects of one's life. College should open new doors for us to a broader, richer life, spiritually, intellectually and socially. If instead it has given us merely a rather pleasant four years, some exploitable connections and a training for our future trade or professions, someone has failed. Let not the failure be yours.

50

Self-Control

And

Self-Expression

FROM two disparate sources, our generation has received new confirmation of an ancient insight into the nature of man. The ancient insight is found, of course, in the Bible: *Kee yetzer lev ha-adam ra mine-urav,* "For the imagination of man's heart is evil from his youth." (Genesis 6:5) These rather cryptic words of the Torah imply that deep within the nature of man there swarm aberrant impulses to evil. In the flush of nineteenth century optimism and a touching faith in the inevitability of progress in human affairs, this sober view of human nature was dismissed from mind. How did Coué put it in the twenties? "Every day, in every way, I am getting better and better."

As man's faith in God waned, his faith in man grew apace. Then there came the tragic awakening of two World Wars, and following in the wake of World War II, an appalling revelation of the unspeakable bestiality of which modern men were capable. In decades to come, when all the living witnesses to the slaughter of the six million will have gone, future generations will simply refuse to believe the credibility of the record, so ghastly revealing is it of the ferocity of which men are capable.

But long before 1939, students of the human soul, led by

Freud, were telling us that just beneath the civilized surface there slumber mighty impulses towards destructiveness and towards self-gratification which tug at the restraints set up by society, and seek to cast them aside.

Thus, both bitter experience and modern theoretical insight have joined to confirm a bit of ancient understanding. Indeed, it is upon that insight, more often sensed than expressed, that all education, all morals, all culture and all religion are made possible. Education is possible only through control, concentration and the restraining of the impulse for immediate gratification. Just as the child must learn control of his physical functions—a long and difficult process—so must he learn to hold in check his psychological impulses, if he is to be educated. Without discipline, at first external and then internalized, no learning would be possible. What is true of education is no less true of all other creative aspects of civilization.

And yet, in our time, it is being dinned into our ears that the virtues of self-restraint, self-discipline and self-control are hopelessly old-fashioned. In an almost infinite number of ways, it is proposed as self-evident truth that virtually anything can be fun. The skills we once thought took hours of hard, concentrated work to acquire are now supposed to be readily available the "fun way"— the fun way to learn how to play the piano, the easy way to speak a language, etc. I wonder what real pianists and linguists would say about that. Fun is the final motivation. Anything that yields fun is intrinsically worthwhile. Or, somewhat more elegantly, this philosophy is conveyed in the notion that the highest mode of living is self-expression. I ask, which self shall I express? The impulse that seeks nothing but pleasure, the aggressive, destructive impulses, the impulse to inertia? Or, the creative, aspiring, outreaching self whose fulfillment requires restraint, self-discipline and self-denial. Consult the biographies of the great creative people in the world on the agonies of the flesh and spirit entailed in the creative process. Moses on Mt. Sinai ate no bread and drank no water for forty days, a potent symbol of the self-denial demanded if one is to scale the spiritual heights.

In a word, we live in a permissive culture in which, more and more, we lose the power to say no to our importunate impulses, to our friends and to the modes of our society: "Be a good fellow and come along." The most unpopular word in the language is no. And who, these days, wants to be unpopular when popularity is regarded as the highest goal towards which man can strive.

The perils, to ourselves, our own character and integrity, the perils of self-indulgence to our society are plain and require no reiteration.

I do not apologize for the fact that Judaism numbers more negative commandments—more Thou Shalt Nots—than positive commandments. Jewish character, achievement and spirituality were forged by the strength of inner discipline and restraint. Judaism arose as a protest against a paganism with its invitation to self-abandonment and sensuality. A totally permissive Judaism in which the element of the forbidden has vanished, has ceased to be Judaism in everything but name. Perhaps the finest contribution we can presently make as Jews to our society is the example of a life of moderation buttressed by inner discipline and control. At least no one can live an authentic Jewish life without knowing the strength and grace of control and restraint.

Who
Speaks
To
Us
In
The
Bible?

51

SOMEONE once wryly dubbed the Bible, "The best-seller nobody reads." To that ironic characterization, I am inclined to add: and the book hardly anyone understands. The obstacles in the path of a real grasp of the Bible need hardly be enumerated. It is a book that comes from an ancient world whose way of thinking, feeling and expression, as well as whose basic concepts on the fundamental issues of life, must often appear impenetrable to even the perceptive modern reader. Above all, it makes the claim of being the Word of God, a claim that strikes many these days as quite unfathomable.

And yet, despite the barriers, there is no real coming to terms with Judaism, or the Jewish people, for that matter, without at least some resolution of our attitude towards the Bible. Without it, Judaism is no more conceivable than Hamlet without the Prince of Denmark. Directly or indirectly, the whole vast stream of sacred Jewish literature takes its rise in the Bible much as a mighty river and all its tributaries find their source in some spring or series of springs high in the mountains. No less significantly, the basic ideas and practices of the Jewish religion are forever rooted in the Book of Books. Look at it how you will, the meaning, function and relevance of Judaism for ourselves and our times must, in good measure, hinge upon our attitude towards the book that forms its permanent base.

Men have gone, and still go, to the Bible in quest of various things. For some, it is ancient literature, to be read, enjoyed and evaluated by essentially the same literary standards that apply to all literature, ancient or modern. For some, it is an indispensable source for the knowledge of the history of ancient Israel and its relationships to its contemporary neighbors. For others, it is a source book for an insight into ancient sociology, folk-lore, religion, economics and anthropology with emphasis on the adjective "ancient." These hardly begin to exhaust the range of purposes that draw people to the Bible. While none of these approaches are invalid per se, they are basically extraneous to the authentically Jewish approach.

If, let us say, the Bible is regarded simply as literature then, in all truth, we must admit that there are innumerable works and passages in the ancient literature, to say nothing of the great works of subsequent generations, that can readily match the vigor and beauty of both biblical prose and poetry.

The Odes of Sappho and the Song of Songs, the Book of Job and Sophocles' Oedipus trilogy, for example, stand essentially on the same literary level. As for ancient history, Herodotus is certainly no less reliable than, say, the Books of Samuel. For the folklorist, ancient Canaanite literature (called Ugartic), is every whit as fascinating as the folk tales of Genesis. Clearly, legitimate as these particular, special approaches to the Bible may be they are essentially irrelevant to any serious quest for its Jewish contemporary

199

meaning and relevance. They certainly do not even presume to correspond to the essential thrust of the Bible itself, and that can be summed up in the single Hebrew word, Torah. And Torah means "teaching."

The Bible, then, is meant to be none of the things enumerated above but rather, teaching—God's instruction to the man of Israel, how to live with himself, with fellowman, and with God. Everything in it from cover to cover, what we ordinarily call legend, myth, history, law, parable, poetry, prophecy, all of it is intended to serve this purpose, and no other. If its tales are told, as they are, with unsurpassable economy, if its poetry is majestically uplifting, its history often stirring, so be it. But its authors never consciously sought any of these effects. They wrote essentially with one purpose, to record the divine teaching that it might be "for an inheritance of the congregation of Jacob."

I use the word "write," but actually centuries before the Torah was written down, it was available only in the form of oral tradition, spoken tales, sagas and poems. The process of literary composition came much later with, of course, later additions and variant versions woven into a single fabric of text which modern scholars have sought to unravel through complex systems of analysis.

And, now, what of the Bible's central claim: "And the Lord spoke unto Moses," "and the word of God came to Jeremiah," etc. If, as some insist, these words are to be taken in their strict literalness, as if Moses, say, was God's amanuensis, taking down divine dictation, then, for a whole host of reasons the claim must be disallowed. (I assume that in this skeptical age, these reasons need not be elaborated.)

But if that is the end of the matter, what are we then to

make of the fact, ever-increasingly made plain and certain by all modern biblical research, that the Bible is a unique book, that in its central concepts, its vision of man's relationship to God, its understanding of the nature of religion, it stands distinctly apart from all ancient literature, despite all parallels and surface resemblances? How shall we explain the irrefutable creative originality of the Bible, stamped on its every page? What if, as is the case, there are no direct, immediate antecedents of the basic biblical ideas, and the latter represent rather a kind of evolutionary leap?

Must we not then look carefully again at the biblical text and posit a process, mysterious to be sure, in which communication between God and man took place. Certainly not a process involving words but a seeing, even a hearing and an understanding on the part of man that transcends the normal limits of these experiences. This transcendent experience on the part of the authors of the Bible, say, the prophets, is not to be doubted. Out of this meeting with God—how else can we denominate it?—the prophets distilled their words. The words then are theirs, the vocabulary of their times, but the experience out of which they emerged is an expression of God. All communication, even human communication, is a two-fold process, a speaking and a listening, a revelation and an understanding. The articulation of such listening and understanding into human speech is never perfect. Even Moses, the Talmud says, could not enter the final gate of wisdom.

Sometimes, through the words of the prophets one catches the echo of the voice of God more clearly than at other times. Sometimes it appears with a faint remoteness. The ancient sages of Israel acknowledged as much when they

201

said that the words of the Torah are rich in some places and poor in others.

Let me sum up the basic attitude towards which I have been driving in this letter. The Torah is not the words of God but it is the Word of God. Without God's self-revelation on the one hand and, on the other, without the surpassing of the familiar, **the known,** and the traditional on the part of the prophets, the extraordinary amalgam of the human and divine we call the Bible, is inconceivable.

The Bible's Contemporary Relevance

52

IN MY previous letter I arrived at the conclusion that a modern man can well regard the Bible as the distillation by a group of extraordinary men of their transcendent experience of a genuine confrontation with God. That conclusion will serve us now as a starting point.

Granted that the Torah is the articulation in human terms and in the setting of its own times of a series of such experiences, how does that concern me here and now? Am I being addressed when I read the Bible or listen to the reading of the Torah? Or to put the question in a simple, familiar phrase, what is the contemporary relevance of the Bible?

It will be recalled that I characterized the Bible as divine teaching, nothing more, nothing else. If that is so, if there is embedded in it inextricably an element of the divine, then it follows that such teaching as it contains, must be permanently valid and relevant. This claim is both implicit and explicit in the Bible itself and, of course, is the presupposition on which the entire Jewish religious tradition is based.

But immediately, the critical mind asks, how can that be? Do not all things change and grow, so that "time makes ancient good uncouth?" Do not growing knowledge, changing conditions and deepening insights compel us to abandon old concepts and ancient standards whether these latter be expressed in words, faith or practice? Was it not Heraclitus who said, a very long time ago, "nothing is permanent but change; all is flux." How then can we speak of the permanent relevance and validity of the Bible?

I raise this rather obvious question because before we can listen seriously to what the Torah has to say, we must be *prepared* to listen. If we were to be predisposed in advance, as we would be if this question remained unanswered, to dismiss a book as ancient as the Bible as outmoded, an impenetrable barrier would have been raised between it and ourselves. This letter is meant to clear away that roadblock and indicate why the Torah is as pertinent today as ever in the past.

Like all generalization, that of Heraclitus has its element of exaggeration. In its essential lines, the human condition does not change. Man is still born of woman, he struggles, hopes, loves, rejoices, begets, achieves, suffers and dies. The basic human experiences vary little from generation to generation. Much the same desires and needs that motivated our ancestors still move us: the desires of the flesh, the search for wisdom, the yearning for love and human companionship, the quest for God—these are from everlasting to everlasting. And it is precisely these situations that the Bible has etched for us in lines so deep and true as to forever call forth recognition and response.

The story of Adam and Eve with its lessons of man's loss of innocence, his desire to be all powerful (like God), the struggle for domination between him and the woman, is as eternal as the situation it depicts. Of course, there never was an Adam and there never was an Eve, but every man now goes through the experience of Adam, and every woman goes through the experience of Eve. What was it that Goethe said? "That which never existed, never grows old and never dies." It is no wonder that those who probe the psychological nature of man, refer again and again to the biblical tale of Adam and Eve, and by it seek to confirm their own theories, much as Freud sought to illuminate some of his own by references to Sophocle's Oedipus, King of Thebes. Forgive the repetition at this point, but I do trust that even this scanty allusion to the import of the Adam and Eve story suffices to undergird our insistence that this tale like all others in the Bible was not meant to entertain or delight, but to teach. As a lesson it might be entitled "The Nature of Man and His Destiny."

The permanent relevance of the Bible consists, however, not alone of its eternally valid insights into the human condition. Always in the Jewish tradition, the Bible has been a living book. That is to say, its meaning has never been regarded as permanently and immutably fixed. Almost from its very inception there was a living oral tradition as to how the Bible was to be interpreted. Always, the Jew saw the Bible through the glass of this tradition of interpretation. Literalism was never a habit of the Jewish mind. This license to interpret, the sages find in the Torah itself. They developed highly complex rules of interpretation and, as often as not, they disagreed among themselves on how a particular verse, phrase, or even word, ought to be understood. Generation after generation did not hesitate to offer its own interpretations. The process known as *midrash* has, in a sense, not ceased even in our day.

Obviously, when a man interprets a text he cannot help

but see it through his own mind as conditioned by the needs and currents of thought of his own time. Thus, thanks to this on-going process of *midrash*, the Bible retained its freshness and relevance, what one might call its presentness.

Does this presentness still abide? Can one still hear the word of God when we read for example, "And the Lord said unto Moses, speak unto the children of Israel and say unto them"? Whatever in the Torah that speaks to us with the force of irresistible command, whatever in the Torah reveals truth to us, whatever moves us to justice, loving-kindness and compassion, whatever overcomes our need for rationalization and enables us to see our weakness and folly, whatever in the Torah bestirs in us a need for seeking a sense of the nearness of God—that, for us, is the word of God. That is *mitzvah*-command. To be sure, not every line will do this and not every time we turn to read the Bible will it speak to us in so significant a way. But there are occasions, there are hours, and there are moments, when its word will come to us with transforming power and passion. For, to repeat, communication is a two-sided process. We must be prepared, we must be in the mood to really listen if genuine communication is to take place.

Now, the view of the Bible set forth here does not claim to be Orthodox, which insists that every word of Scripture is literally the precise word of God. But I do insist that, all theories aside, the attitude I have described is how the Bible was actually regarded in Jewish tradition. Moreover, it is a view that can recommend itself to a modern Jew who would come to terms in an intelligible, meaningful way with the Book that is the unfailing source of our Jewish being and tradition.

206

**The
Bible
And
Modern
Knowledge**

FOR MINDS that have been touched by some sophistication there is a serious stumbling block that must be removed before the Bible can be taken earnestly. I have reference to the fact that a literal reading of the Holy Writings reveals, at various points, patent contradictions between the findings of modern knowledge and statements in Scripture. While they need not be enumerated, one or two ought to be instanced, so that you know specifically the kind of mental collision that is bound to occur when, say, a young person hears for the first time of the theory of evolution and then recalls the biblical account of the creation of the world and of man. Or, he contrasts the biblical story of the origin of a multiplicity of languages (the story of the Tower of Babel) and what modern linguistics has to teach on the subject.

At the risk of tiresome reiteration, I must again remind you of my insistence that just as the Bible was never meant to be a book of history, per se, neither was it meant to be a book of science designed to meet curiosity on the physical nature and origin of things. One of the great blunders of the past, even on the part of otherwise brilliant and perceptive minds, Jewish as well as non-Jewish, was to regard

such stories as actual, incontrovertible accounts of the physical origins and processes of nature. In the fantastically
ingenious effort to reconcile the Bible with the findings of
science, it was completely overlooked that the two stood on
totally different levels, poles apart in both method and purpose. There are still, alas, those who follow this dead-end
road, as pointless as it is fruitless. Perhaps you have heard
the fantastic notion, developed in an effort to harmonize
the first chapter of Genesis with the teachings of geology,
that when the former says "it was evening and it was
morning, one day," it really means an epoch, not a day of
twenty-four hours. I would not waste your time, nor mine,
in refuting notions that possess no more substance than a
soap bubble.

Instead, I would rather engage you in drawing out some
of the lessons the Torah would teach in its story of the
creation of the world and the Tower of Babel, to stick to
our two original examples.

Open your Bible and read the first chapter of Genesis
again. You will note at once that the story shows virtually
no interest in the process whereby the earth, the sun, man,
fish, etc., were created. On this score, all it has to say is:
"And God said, let there be . . . And God said, let the waters
swarm . . . And God said, let the earth bring forth." How
these things come to be, in response to God's command,
apparently does not interest the author. The only beings
whose process of creation does concern the author are man
and woman: "And the Lord God fashioned man dust from
the earth, and He breathed into his nostrils a living soul..."
(Genesis 2:7) This sudden interest is certainly not fortui-
tous. For it is man, his nature and destiny before God, that

208

forms the focus of the author's concern. Man is compounded of dust not, as in ancient Semitic myth, out of some part or excrescence of the body of a God. Since he is made of dust, hence his subsequent mortality. Withal, he is created in the image of God, hence, the unique relationship to God in which he stands. Then God, as creative power, calls forth all existence, and climaxes it with the creation of man. Creation displays harmony and order, balance and structure. Opposites are brought into harmonious balance. "And it was evening and it was morning, one day." Darkness and light together constitute a day just as, subsequently, the waters above the firmament and the waters below it are divided by the latter so that they do not clash. The scheme is followed consistently and reaches its acme with the creation of man whose counterpart is the woman to be a "helpmeet unto him." As each day passes, God pronounces judgment upon His work: "And God saw that it was good." All is harmony and peace. This is God's purpose, one that is later, of course, to be subverted by the willfulness of man.

I submit that, seen in this light, the story is no more out of kilter with the theory of evolution than a painting of Niagara Falls can be said to contradict an engineer's account of how much electrical energy can be generated from the flow of its water. For reduced to its essential minimum, the teaching of the story is two-fold: God is the creative power who stands behind all manifestations of existence, and His purpose was (and is) that of establishing harmony and peaceful order between all that exists. Genesis chapter one, then, is a religious understanding and vision of life, no more subject to contradiction by science, present or future, than the experience of genuine human love is contradicted by the discovery of the existence of male and female hormones.

Let us briefly turn now to the story of the Tower of Babel (Genesis chapter 2, verses 1-9). God's mixing up the languages of men (verse 8) and His scattering them over the face of all the earth (verse 9) are obviously meant to describe divine punishment of men's presumption to reach heaven by means of the tower they had built. In a word, man's attempt to reach heaven and become God is a piece of insufferable arrogance that must bring disaster. That is the essential thrust of the story—man must not seek to become God. Any such effort must end in calamity. For what else, if not a calamity, is the result of man not being able to understand his fellowman because of difference in language? What else, but disaster, is the breaking up of the primal solidarity that once invited all men?

Of course, linguistics gives a totally different account of the spread of languages and their familiar relationship one to another. But again, the biblical story is not meant to be a straightforward factual description. It is an expression of religio-moral judgment as disparate from the former as a poem about a rose is from a botanist's classification and description.

To both stories, there is a biblical sequel, and I cannot conclude without some slight reference to it. At the end of time, the Bible tells us, creation will attain God's original purpose. Peace and harmony will be established (see Isaiah chapter 2, verse 4 and chapter 11, verses 6-9). The time will come when all men will understand each other and, in their common understanding, will call upon the one God, and worship Him together in unity (Zephaniah 3:9).

210

These two examples, I trust, will suffice to indicate that while modern knowledge (in my interpretation I have drawn on modern biblical scholarship) may help us to understand the Bible it cannot, in the nature of the case, discredit it. Sophistication may temporarily put stumbling blocks in our way towards any serious appreciation of the Bible. But the time must come when we pass beyond sophistication towards some growing wisdom.

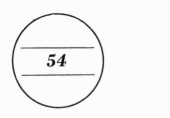

Judaism

And

Christianity

AN increasing number of colleges are offering courses in comparative religion. It is more than likely that such a course is given by an instructor who, for all his efforts to maintain academic objectivity, is essentially committed to Christianity and, hence, presents the section dealing with Judaism from a Christian point of view. From that standpoint, Judaism is regarded as a religion whose historical function was fulfilled in paving the way for Christianity. The latter is conceived by Christians as the culmination and final flowering of Judaism, as a dispensation that brought to final completion and culmination all that was eternally true and good in its predecessor. Thus, it has been attempted to prove that the essential seeds of the doctrine of Christianity are already to be found in biblical Judaism.

There is enough truth in this claim to lend it an air of verisimilitude. The borrowings of Christianity from Judaism are enormous. But what is ignored are the differences that separate the two faiths, differences that are so vast and deep as to sunder them into distinctive, not parallel, approaches to the basic issues of God, the world and man.

In this letter, I shall confine myself to sketching the basic differences, and shall refrain from any argument as to their respective merits. (The latter I regard as a largely futile exercise.) I do think it is important that an intelligent Jew be aware of the differences that set off Judaism from Christianity as well as the elements the two faiths hold in common.

All versions of Christianity, except Unitarianism which Christians themselves do not consider a Christian sect, agree on regarding the life and character of Jesus as embodying a unique revelation of God. For the Christian, he is the son of God whether this term is taken almost literally, as it is by the devout Catholic, or fairly symbolically, as it is by the liberal Protestant. The saying of Jesus, "None comes to the Father, except through the son," plays a key role in Christian thought and practice.

This notion of the unique intermediary between man and God is completely foreign to Judaism. Indeed, the whole concept of a being who is both man and God is utterly alien to our religion.

For Christianity, Jesus' function in the world was redemptive. His death was a sacrificial offering, ordained by God, and intended to offer mankind atonement for its sins. Hence, the familiar designation in Christianity of Jesus as the Saviour. Without this doctrine of vicarious atonement, the whole purpose of Jesus' life and death becomes problematical.

There is no figure in Judaism whose life or death is interpreted in this light. Judaism does not stand or fall with the doctrine of vicarious atonement. Indeed, the latter could not, in the nature of the case, ever achieve the key role it does in Christianity. Only a doctrine of original sin—the notion that all men, by their very being, participate in the sin of Adam—requires a universal saviour sent to offer

213

them atonement for that sin. Judaism has no doctrine of original sin.

Christianity, in its ritual aspects, revolves around the birth and death of Jesus. (The two great Christian religious festivals are, of course, Christmas and Easter.) The great religious festivals of Judaism revolve around either the great, significant events in the ancient life of Israel, or around the universal themes of judgment and atonement. Contrast, for example, the meaning of Passover and the meaning of Easter.

It is not, however, in doctrine and ritual alone that Judaism and Christianity differ. In the latter, man achieves salvation through faith in the supernatural, redemptive character of Jesus. ("Believe," says Jesus, "and ye shall be saved.") Hence, the recitation of the creed is a central feature of the Christian liturgy. In Judaism, salvation is achieved through deeds, the *mitzvot* which a man performs. Nowhere in the vast body of sacred Jewish writings will you find the idea that faith, per se, guarantees salvation.

Indeed, while the idea of an afterlife did enter Judaism in the rabbinic period, the original cast of Judaism as a this-worldly religion was never completely overcome. In normative Judaism, its highest expression was never regarded as an ascetic denial of either the goods or the pleasures of this world. Christianity, on the other hand, tended in its classical version (Catholicism) to regard the ascetic as the person who had attained the highest spiritual level; hence, the vows of poverty and chastity of the Catholic clergy. The saint was he who had foresworn all worldly goods. This asceticism, it ought be noted, far from being a distortion of the way of life preached by Jesus and Paul, is actually its fulfillment. Recall Jesus' saying: "Sooner

214

can a camel pass through the eye of a needle than a rich man can enter heaven." Or, consider his counsel to his would-be disciples: "Sell or give away what you have and follow me." Paul taught that it was better for man "to burn, rather than marry" but that if he could not abide that state, he might marry. Marriage, then, in early Christianity, was regarded as a concession to the weakness of the flesh. Judaism, on the other hand, regards marriage and the propagation of the race as a *mitzvah*.

Historically, the parting of the ways between the two faiths took place not on any of these issues which were just beginning to germinate at the time of the rise of Christianity, but rather on an altogether different question. Was Jesus the Messiah? The Messiah in Jewish thought, it must be recalled, would be he who would bring redemption to Israel, and to the world, in the here and now. And redemption meant freedom and peace. Obviously, the Jewish answer, in keeping with its own teachings, had to be that Jesus was not the Messiah. Clearly, freedom and peace for both Israel and the world were still far off. Those who followed Jesus, and subsequently joined the church, transferred redemption to the afterlife and to a second coming of Jesus. For the Christian, the denouement of human history has already taken place; for the Jew it is yet to take place.

While this account is by no means exhaustive, it does indicate that only the simple-minded can accept the idea that essentially Christianity and Judaism are at one on the basic issues. Actually, in the course of its development, Christianity which began as a Jewish sect was infused with a number of Greek and pagan elements which stand in total contrast to the teachings of Judaism.

If, in this letter, I have emphasized the disparate aspects

215

of the two faiths, it is because the widespread use of the phrase "the Judaeo-Christian" tradition has given rise to the erroneous notion that the two religions are essentially identical. They are not. Once the historic parting of the ways took place between Christianity and Judaism each followed its own development. An understanding and mutual tolerance between the two, a consummation devoutly to be hoped for, can come not by a submerging of differences but rather by their acceptance. Only on this basis is a dialogue between Judaism and Christianity possible. In practical terms, that means that the church will have to stop looking upon us as potential candidates for conversion. Here and there, a truly liberal Christian leader has suggested as much. But it will be a long, a very long, time before the church changes its historic posture towards Judaism.

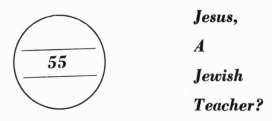

Jesus,
A
Jewish
Teacher?

OCCASIONALLY, I get this question from a college student (fresh perhaps from serious discussion on religion with a Christian college mate): "Why can't Jews accept Jesus as a teacher of lofty ethics, much as they accept any of the prophets or sages of ancient Israel? After all, why must he who was born of the community of Israel be permanently excluded from the luminous roster of the great Jewish teachers?" The question has been posed often enough, and not by college students alone, to merit a serious, considered answer.

In the Christian tradition, Jesus occupies a unique position, one that Judaism cannot concede to any man without repudiating its own very essence, e.g. that God cannot become man and that man cannot become God. To include Jesus, in the light of that fact, in the synagogue is to create endless confusion. When we quote him as an authority, as we quote say, Amos or Hillel, the impression would be inevitably that the synagogue had accepted Jesus, not simply as another Jewish teacher, but rather as the Messiah, the Saviour and the son of God. Obviously, all these Christian concepts of Jesus are totally alien to us. History, and, for

217

that matter, the living present are not overcome that simply.

This is the least of the obstacles. There are more basic considerations. I am convinced that in his own mind Jesus saw himself as something more than a rabbi, a teacher and an expounder of the Jewish tradition. There is incontrovertible evidence that in his own mind Jesus saw himself as the Messiah about to usher in the Kingdom of God. In that Kingdom, he would play a most prominent role— "sitting on the right hand of God." Judaism rejected, and continues to reject, the idea that the Messiah has already come. By his own claim, and failure to fulfill that claim, Jesus put himself, as far as the synagogue is concerned, in the category of false Messiahs. To disregard this aspect of his character, is to disregard what was central in Jesus' own teaching.

As for that teaching, aside from the role he believed he was fulfilling, here too, there are a number of insuperable problems. Jesus taught and preached, as no other rabbi of his time, or subsequent times, for that matter. Always, his teaching was put in the form of, "I say unto you." That is, his authority and that of his teaching derived from his own personal status as a supernatural being. No rabbi ever taught in that fashion. Always the sages of Israel based their doctrine not on their position, no matter how exalted, but rather on the authority of the Torah. They interpreted the Torah just as any scholar might do. Hence, the differences of opinion so abundant in the Talmud. No one could speak with final, absolute authority in Judaism. If someone claimed to have direct communication from Heaven, as occasionally happened, he was promptly told that no attention was to be paid to heavenly voices. In this regard, Jesus clearly stands at an unbridgeable remove from all his Jewish teachers.

But, perhaps, the most important consideration that permanently excludes Jesus from the synagogue is the very substance of so much of his doctrine. We refer here to his ethical doctrine, the basis on which it is proposed to incorporate him into the synagogue.

I have already intimated that ancient Judaism exhibits a fairly wide spectrum of moral ideas, including some extreme views. These latter are distinctly minority views, and had little bearing on the formation of the mainstream of Jewish thought. To borrow an example from another area: One rabbi of the Talmud was of the opinion that "Israel has no Messiah. King Hezekiah had been intended as the Messiah." This lone, solitary voice was completely drowned out by the persistent tradition of Jewish messianism.

In many of his ethical teachings, Jesus represents a decidedly minority viewpoint, one completely at variance with the main thrust of Jewish teaching. Jesus was an extreme pacifist: "Resist not evil." "Turn the other cheek." Normative Judaism teaches that evil ought be resisted, and to turn the other cheek in the face of unwarranted assault is to encourage evil. Jesus taught that a man should love his enemies. Judaism never made such unrealistic, utopian, impossible demands. So then, in many respects the ethic of Jesus is at variance with that of the mainstream of Jewish tradition.

These are some of the considerations that the recurrent plea to reclaim Jesus for the Jewish people must meet. Despite the fact that he is reported to have said, "I have not been sent but to the lost sheep of the House of Israel," actually, in historical perspective, his role was directed to the nations, not to Israel. What he had to teach the nations in the ethical sphere had been taught to Israel before him by prophets and sages.

History cannot be undone. History has made the man from Nazareth the central figure of a faith distinct, in basic respects, from that of Judaism. To the devout Christian, a view of Jesus other than that of the "son of God," is blasphemous. We Jews, God knows, have enough problems. Must we add to them by a public demythologization of Jesus? What good would it do anyone, Jew or Christian?

Toynbee
On
Judaism
And
Christianity

LATTERLY, I have been burning the midnight oil with Arnold Toynbee's ten volume *Study of History*. Toynbee has come to be regarded as a modern Christian prophet and more than once *Life* magazine has given his massive work enthusiastic attention. A one volume summary of the first four volumes of his book was something of a best seller a few years back. Obviously, the work's interest goes far beyond the narrow circle of professional students of history. For, like the ancient prophets, Toynbee apportions praise and blame, he blesses and castigates people's ideas and institutions. And, like the prophets, he attempts to chart the future of man's destiny.

My own approach to this monumental work, certain to be consulted by generations of students, is by way of the path I know best: Jewish history. How do Jews and Judaism fare in Toynbee's work? For all his recognition of positive Jewish contributions to civilization, Toynbee puts us, our religion and our ethic in an extremely unflattering light. Not even the longest "Letter" could take up and analyze, point by point, Toynbee's deprecatory judgments on Jews and Judaism. That would require a book of hundreds of pages. Here, I would like to touch upon one or two central issues.

Toynbee writes: "(The Jews) brooding on a talent which they had perversely sterilized by hiding it in the earth, they rejected the still greater treasure which God offered them in the coming of Jesus of Nazareth." Plainly, this is the conventional traditional Christian position that Jesus represented a fuller and richer revelation of God than that which had once been vouchsafed to the Jews. An infinitude of zeal, learning and ingenuity have been expended by Christian theologians in attempting to prove the unprovable: that Jesus represented a greater treasure. How does one measure, objectively, as a historian should measure, matters of faith? Toynbee's judgment is an act of faith, something that is everybody's prerogative, but it is certainly no soberly reasoned historical opinion.

There is yet another judgment of Toynbee's that cries out for critical scrutiny. As a historian, Toynbee is painfully aware of the long, doleful record of persecution and fanaticism that is part of the history of organized Christendom. He cites it and documents it again and again. But his moral embarrassment is somewhat relieved by as neat an intellectual dodge as I have met in a lifetime of study. Here it is: The ethos of Christianity, its own native vision and outlook upon life, according to Toynbee, is one of gentleness and love: its intolerance it inherited from Judaism. I would ask but one question of Toynbee: If Christianity's authentic ethos is gentleness and love, why did it take over from Judaism—if it did—an element so incompatible with its own spirit? Did not Christianity reject a number of elements in Judaism: for example, the Law? Why then did it seemingly borrow (?) so fulsomely what Toynbee terms a

222

"Judaically fanatical ferocity?" The question ought lead one to suspect there may have been sources other than Judaism from which historic Christianity borrowed its intolerance.

These are a few of the sparks—or are they flames of indignation?—that reading Toynbee has ignited.